## Endorsements

"Pastor Tommy Reid put a lifetime of thoughts and lessons of a dreamer into this book. Something worked itself into this man when he was a young boy which wove eternity into his very DNA. He now brings to us the inner life and thoughts of what it means to dream, to wrestle with a dream, and to see the dream into reality.

Walking alongside of Tommy Reid has been one of the blessings of my life. He is a dreamer who partners with Heaven to see dreams birthed into everyone around him.

In this manuscript, he is joined by his daughter, Aimee Reid Sych, to whom he has passed his ability to dream and understand the dreams of the next generation."

Reverend Robert Stearns
Founder and President of Eagles Wings

---

"Best-selling author, Tommy Reid has masterfully done it again. This time, he tells us to discover how to dream God's dream and to learn how to see that dream transformed into reality.

*How to Live Out of a Dream* has the power to ignite your dreams long before you reach the last chapter. I believe it will be one of the most important works you have ever read."

Bishop Levy Knox
Bishop Living Word Christian Center
Mobile, Alabama

---

# HOW TO *Live* OUT OF A *Dream*

## BY
## TOMMY REID
## & AIMEE REID-SYCH

Heritage Publishing & Distributing
*of Central FL. Inc.*
*~ Publishing & Print Management ~*
Info@heritagepd.com
www.heritagepd.com

All Scripture references are noted in the Bibliography on page 144.

Library of Congress Control Number: 2013943051
ISBN 978-0-578-12598-5

Published by: **COVnet Ministries**
1st Printing: July 2013
2nd Printing: May 2014
3rd Printing: November 2014

Contact:
Thomas F. Reid
COVnet Ministries
3210 Southwestern Boulevard
Orchard Park, New York 14127
e-mail: tommyreid@dreammydestiny.com
e-mail: treidcovnet@gmail.com

Fulfillment & Distribution Services provided by:
**KAIROS Media**
3210 Southwestern Boulevard
Orchard Park, New York 14127
1-800-51WINGS

Printed in USA

*All Printing & Book Services provided by:*
Heritage Publishing & Distributing
*of Central FL. Inc.*
buz.swyers@heritagepd.com
www.heritagepd.com

# How to live out of a Dream

## Table of Contents

## VI - HOW TO LIVE OUT OF A DREAM

## DREAMERS IN HISTORY

## A LEGACY Of DREAMS
### ~ perspective from the next generation ~
~
**Rev. Aimee L. Reid-Sych**
"Commanding Your Post!"

# VIII - HOW TO LIVE OUT OF A DREAM

# FOREWORD

## How to Live Out of a Dream
### Bishop Levy H. Knox

In this book, **How to Live Out of a Dream**, Bishop Thomas Reid has masterfully done it again. The best-selling author of instant classics such as, **The Exploding Church** and **The Kingdom Now but Not Yet**, takes you on an amazing spiritual journey within. Not only will you discover how to dream a "God dream," but you'll learn how to see that dream transformed into reality.

Bishop Reid has the depth of character and graciousness of spirit to reveal how one can reach into the world of the unseen and bring it into the world of the seen. He shares in this powerful literary work how the world inside of you can change the world around you so that it becomes exactly like the world within you. Your job is to move your feet in the direction of your dream and expect that it will meet you… and it will!

Bishop Reid is a dreamer. He has always been a dreamer. In Buffalo, NY, over 14 churches were created out of his dream. All over the world, there are ministries and churches that were first of all, only a dream in his heart. I believe in dreams. My wife Lady Delia was confined to a wheelchair for twenty-two-and-one-half years. She dreamed a "God dream" of walking again. Hundreds of thousands of people throughout the world have watched the video that went viral and have witnessed her getting out of the wheelchair by the sovereign, miraculous power of God. "The powers of the age to come invaded this present age." The invisible

Kingdom of Heaven invaded this time/space world. Today she walks and runs, and like the man in the scripture, she even leaps! Lady Delia's walking was once only a dream in her heart, but now we are living out of a dream transformed into reality.

Within each of us lies an unquenchable desire to have dreams of a better life, better family, a better world; an idea longing to be nourished, cherished, launched and completed. Our deepest desire is to see the dream manifested – to carefully and patiently watch it unfold, and to present it to those who will benefit from it and experience the joy of the dream.

The moment you start to dream, everything shifts: purpose, focus, passion and peace return to your life. Eyes sparkle, energy explodes, inspiration and creativity flow and our days become supported by confidence, power and new possibilities. I'm convinced that a dream from God will lift people up and pour mastery, courage and light into a world that is aching for heroism. So many of the world's problems and perplexities are symptoms of dreams unfulfilled and undone and the lack of true dreamers. Dreams from God will bring solutions to the two worlds in which we live – the world within us and the world around us.

Jesus said the Kingdom of Heaven is within you. He demonstrated that Kingdom within on the stormy Sea of Galilee as a ship was tossed by a raging squall so strong that the big, brave fishermen in the boat with Jesus feared for their lives. At the same time, Jesus was asleep. He slept because the world inside of Him was a world of peace. When they awakened Him, they questioned Jesus and what they perceived to be His lack of concern for them. Jesus, in turn, questioned their lack of faith. But when He commanded the storm to be still, He took the world of peace within Him and redefined the world around Him until the world around Him became exactly like the world inside of Him.

The world of peace inside of Jesus was so much powerful than the world around Him. To Bishop Reid, dreams are like that. They are more powerful than the world around you.

In 2 Kings 4, the prophet of God came to the house of a woman who had a secret dream. The prophetic spirit in the man of God uncovered a deep seated and unspoken dream in the heart of that woman. This book will help you uncover and recognize, not only the secret dream inside of you, but also the reality of that dream. It will stir up a desire in you to create a roadmap to realizing your dreams.

So what is the God dream that is pulling you forward? Whatever it may be, you don't have to take the journey of discovering it alone. Through this book, Bishop Reid will help you to identify, navigate, and transform your dream into reality. Everything you perceive in the physical world has its origin in the invisible world within you – the world where dreams begin. Your connection to the physical reality of God's divine destiny is the dream that God places in your heart.

The Bible says the knowledge of the glory of the Lord shall cover the earth. Glory emanates from another realm that is breaking through into this realm. There is a "thinning" of the veil between this world (seen) and the world to come (unseen). The dream in your heart is a portion of the glory of God that is manifested in our world. Some of you reading this may wonder why your dream is being prolonged. Well, I believe that this is your season of the supernatural. When you are in the right place at the right time, your dream will become reality. Many of you might have to dust off the dream; for some, you just need to keep dreaming; and others, simply dream again. In Genesis 37:5, "Joseph dreamed a dream ...," in Verse 9 "he dreamed yet another dream..." Like Joseph, let God create the reality of the dream in your heart in the world around you.

Although a dream is invisible to physical sight, it is an actual force. When you think and move confidently in the direction of your dream, you cross an invisible boundary. Once you cross this invisible boundary line, all sorts of things begin to happen. Your dream begins to connect with other dreamers who think along the same lines. Dreamers walk toward the future confidently. So keep reaching toward your dream and your dream will become your destiny. It's just as easy to think around the globe as it is to think across the room. It takes no more energy to dream an audacious dream than it does to dream a tiny, safe dream. The only thing between a dream and reality is action. Dream big and don't underestimate your ability to get there!

Bishop Reid has written this book in such a way that anyone can easily comprehend and employ his concepts on how to live their dream and transform it into a living reality from the inside out. From beginning to end, it's like an easy-to-read guide that will take you from where you are right now to the destination of the dream in your heart. He will take you into the unseen world within where dreams begin and show you how to transform those dreams into the visible.

I have been in ministry for over thirty years; the latter twenty-eight of those years have been spent serving as a Senior Pastor. In all that time, never has there been another book concerning how to dream God's dream from conception to maturation that has made such an impact on my life. The clarity and insight within the pages of **How to Live Out of a Dream** has the power to ignite your dreams long before you've reached the last chapter.

I've observed in my life that one of the vital characteristics in having a dream from God is enthusiasm. Enthusiasm becomes a catalyst to your dream. The root word of enthusiasm is entheos, which literally means "God within." A God dream will bring aliveness to your heart as you imagine living in the fulfillment of that dream. So enjoy what I believe will be one of the most important works you have ever read; and of course, dare to dream, dare to believe, and dare to do!

**Dr. Levy H. Knox, Bishop & Founder**
Living Word Christian Center Intl. Ministries
Kingdom Network of Churches International (KNCI)
Opportunity for Unity Ministry Network (OFU)
www.lwccim.com

# PREFACE

## Rev. Robert Stearns

*A*nd it shall come to pass afterward, that I will pour out my spirit upon all flesh; and your sons and your daughters shall prophesy, your old men shall dream dreams, your young men shall see visions: And also upon the servants and upon the handmaids in those days will I pour out my spirit. And it shall come to pass, that whosoever shall call on the name of the Lord shall be delivered: for in mount Zion and in Jerusalem shall be deliverance, as the Lord hath said, and in the remnant whom the Lord shall call.
Joel 2:28-32 (KJV)

The Bible is full of dreams and dreamers. From Jacob's dream of the ladder, to Joseph's dream (which got him into trouble) – to the New Testament Joseph being spoken to in a dream about the child growing inside of Mary, dreamers and their dreams have determined the Scriptural narrative.

Scripture also tells us that dreaming will not end, but rather, that in the "last days," old men will "dream dreams, and young men will see visions."

There is something unique about those who listen to their dreams. There is an openness, a vulnerability – a child-likeness that at the same time has a certain authority to it, like they are able to listen to another world, and help us hear that world too.

Pastor Tommy Reid has, now at 80 years of age, has put a lifetime of thoughts and lessons of a dreamer into this book. Something worked itself into this man when he was a young boy which wove eternity into his very DNA.

Pastor Tommy has been "Pastor" to countless thousands throughout the world. From pastoring the largest church in his denomination as a young man in his 20s, to walking alongside Dr. Yonggi Cho as the great work in Korea began, Tommy Reid has been an integral part of modern church history.

Though the nations have been a part of his life, the families of The Tabernacle and the work of the Lord in Buffalo, NY have always been the central heartbeat of this spiritual father and visionary. The spiritual landscape of Western New York has been permanently impacted by the thousands of lives Pastor has led into the Kingdom and capably and lovingly shepherded. There are churches across the Western NY landscape which his visionary leadership has helped to plant and establish.

Now, he brings to us the inner life and thoughts of what it means to dream, to wrestle with a dream, and to see the dream birthed into reality.

With wisdom, inspiration, and transparency, Pastor invites us to understand that whenever there is a dream, there will be conflict surrounding that dream, for we live in a world where God dreams for so much more for our planet than we currently see. We know from the Scriptures and the witness of the voice of the Spirit in our hearts that God has something better for our world; yet, so much of our world is trapped in places of hurt and brokenness, living far beneath the full potential God has designed for us.

How do we handle this conflict? How do we stand strong in faith when we are "in between" what we see with the eye of our heart and what we see in the natural world around us? How do we do as he does, and enter the winter of our life still believing, still hoping, still dreaming, and not embittered and disillusioned.

More than ever before in our world, we need to be taught and encouraged to hold on to our dreams. We need to partner with the Holy Spirit in seeing His creativity and the heart of God released and the hope of God given fresh place. Pastor invites us to partner with God in hearing and releasing Heaven's dreams into our world. In this, he has led the way for us for the past 65 years of full-time ministry. He is as vibrant and insightful as ever as he pours into this next generation the heart and soul of a dreamer.

In 1993, I was a young man in my 20s, with a dream in my heart of what God wanted to do in and through my life and through Eagles Wings. I had nothing but a dream. I shared that dream with Tommy Reid. This giant who had stood with giants and heard the great dreams of his generation did not think my dream small or unimportant. Rather, he listened, and counseled, and sowed, and believed. Eagles Wings would not have had the foundation it had if it were not for Pastor caring for not only his dreams, but mine as well.

Walking alongside Tommy Reid has been one of the great blessings of my life. He is a genuine lover of God and lover of people. He is a father, a mentor, a teacher, a model, a statesman, a prophet, an apostle, and a friend. He is what a genuine spiritual leader should be; a dreamer who partners with Heaven to see those dreams birthed in the lives of everyone around him.

This book will give you a living understanding on nurturing and manifesting the dreams of God within you from the heart and life of a trusted dreamer. May you be blessed as you read and live it.

**Rev. Robert Stearns**
**Eagles Wings Ministry**

# INTRODUCTION

This is a book that I had to write. In my lifetime I have written three successful books. The first, **The Exploding Church**, became one of America's best selling religious books and thrust this author into a world of speaking at large conventions, being a guest on all of the major Christian networks, and writing for some of the largest religious periodicals.

My life has been one of what most would consider a successful ministry. My first five years of ministry were spent in evangelism throughout the United States and Canada. I then went to Asia for five years of ministry. At 26, I was asked to serve as Pastor of the largest church in my denomination, in Manila, Philippines, following its founder, Dr. Lester Sumrall. At the age of 31, my denomination asked me to go to Korea and work with an unknown Korean pastor by the name of Paul Cho. We immediately became friends and worked together closely for almost a year. While we were with Pastor Cho, the church grew from about 300 people to over 3,000 and soon became the largest church in the world.

Before I left Korea, Paul (now David) Cho asked me to become his co-pastor for the rest of my life. But, I left Korea because I had a calling and a mandate from God to build a ministry in my hometown of Buffalo, NY.

This book is the story of the conflict I experienced between the vision inside of me of the church I was destined to build in Buffalo and the world around me where I was destined by God to plant the church that was inside of me.

After two years of seeing this church inside of me, at the age of 31, I did go to Buffalo to plant the vision inside of me. For the first five years of ministry in Buffalo, it seemed that nothing worked for me. I went from being a success as an evangelist and pastor in Asia to becoming a failure in Buffalo. Needless to say, I was devastated and considered leaving the ministry. But eventually, after two years and continuing to see this church inside me, through a sovereign outpouring of the Holy Spirit in our church, we experienced tremendous growth.

That church was now taking shape. That ministry today has developed a world television network and over the years has built 14 churches which include many para-church ministries in separate locations in the Buffalo area. It has sent scores of preachers and missionaries who were trained in our Bible School to many countries where great missions works have been built. Today, each Sunday, there are several thousand people who worship on our multiple campuses.

To some, that would be success. I don't know how God judges success, but this is the story of the conflict that took place in my heart that led me to where I am today.

I developed a philosophy of life as an eight-year-old child that kept me from totally giving up on life at crucial and challenging times. It has made me who I am today.

Now, as I come to another time of transition in life, I feel I need to tell the world what makes a person succeed in life. I know it works, because it worked for me. I served in Buffalo for over five years without any success. In fact, it appeared that I had totally failed. But, I kept going back to what I believed. Having contracted polio as a child, I became crippled. I was also plagued with a stuttering and stammering tongue.

For these reasons, I decided that I needed to believe in something. Being raised in a Christian home, I did believe in God and even as a child developed a strong faith. But I also needed to believe in myself. That was difficult because of all the preaching I had heard about the wicked heart of man. Was I really worth saving? Was there anything good or valuable inside of me? And yet, in spite of the conflict of belief inside of me, I did believe I was born for something significant.

Gradually as a child, I developed this philosophy that would guide my life. It centered in one amazing truth: "Every man born on this planet was born with purpose and destiny."

I came to believe I was here on this planet with a divine purpose and was a child of destiny. That core value developed as the very center value of everything I believed. When I was in the Philippines with Lester Sumrall, when I was in Korea with Dr. Cho, and when I finally returned to Buffalo, I made it through the good times and the bad with the burning passion of this core value in my heart. I believed I was born for this time with destiny and purpose.

Thinking these thoughts at such a young age and developing my philosophy of life brought me to a belief in a vision for my own life. As I thought and prayed about that vision, I discovered three dreams inside of me. Remember: I was only between eight and ten years of age when I began to think these thoughts and live by this philosophy. After spending long times in prayer at the altars of my Pentecostal church and camp meetings, I came to the conclusion that my life had three separate chapters.

## THE FIRST CHAPTER OF MY LIFE:

I knew I would become a prominent evangelist in spite of my shyness and stuttering. That happened within our first three or four years of evangelistic work traveling with a caravan of vehicles that carried a large tent from city to city for our crusades.

## CHAPTER TWO OF MY LIFE:

In the second chapter in my life, I believed I would go overseas to the mission fields of the world and preach large healing crusades as I told about my healing as a cripple. believed that I would touch nations. In the back of my mind, was even the remote idea that this would result in either building or being a pastor of large churches in major cities of the world.

## CHAPTER THREE OF MY LIFE:

In the heart of this ten-year-old child, was the third or final chapter in my life. I saw myself returning to my hometown of Buffalo to build a large church and establish other churches in that city. That would come because the Lord had prepared for me a seed of a church whose people already had a world vision for missions in their hearts.

I was to discover in this remarkable journey that my life would be one of constant struggle and conflict. Not the kind of conflict that you might think. This conflict would be between the world of my dreams and visions and the world of physical reality around me.

That is the plight of every dreamer. We live in two worlds. The inner world of our destiny and dreams, and the physical world around us that seems to be a contradiction to the world inside of us.

And that is what this book is about. It is the story of my battles between these two worlds. I have never seen a book or a manuscript about this kind of war, yet it is often referred to in the stories of people who have accomplished much.

You see, 1 believe that God has placed dreams and visions in the hearts of His people that are destined by Him to solve every problem of our world. The problems with our world is not the dreams inside of us, but rather that we do not believe those dreams. Instead, too many of us look at the world around us and believe that this is true reality. But, it is the world of vision inside of us that is true reality.

After spending a lifetime dreaming the dreams that God placed in my heart, seeing those dreams develop inside of me, and eventually planting them in the world around me, I made an amazing discovery. Spending a lifetime studying the Word of God concerning the subject of men and women who have dreamed God's dreams, I also discovered that the Bible teaches that the God-dreams we dream were written by God before the foundation of the world.

The scripture tells us in Revelation 17:8: "That there are people whose names are not written in the book of life from the foundation of the world." This scripture also infers that there are those whose destiny was recorded by God before the creation of matter itself. In Hebrews 4:3, the scripture also teaches us that: "Our 'works' were finished from the foundation of the world." In this book, we will discuss several other passages that teach us that our name, or destiny, was established and recorded by God before He ever created a constellation, a star, a planet, a lake, a river, a mountain, or a fragment of the physical universe.

I pray that I can inspire you with this phenomenal truth: that the dream or destiny God placed in your heart was created and recorded by God in His book of life before He made the universe. That is why our destinies even defy the laws of nature.

The destiny of Moses and the children of Israel was so much greater than the physical laws of nature, that even the Red Sea could not stand in their way.

God wrote you and your destiny into His plan and His tapestry for His universe before He made the world. If you believe that, you will realize how important your life and destiny is to the plans of God for His world.

I believe dreams that are in your heart were given to you by God and He placed these dreams and visions in the hearts of His people before the foundation of the world. These people are destined by God to solve every problem of our world.

If that is true, then the problems with our world are not that God has not placed the solutions to those problems inside of us, but rather that we do not believe in those dreams.

**I invite you today to dream with me...**
**Rev. Tommy Reid**

# THE DREAM WORKBOOK
# QUESTIONS FOR THE INTRODUCTION

1. As you think carefully about your life as a child, try to remember the dreams you had. It is suggested that this dream would probably come to you between the 7th and the 10th year of your life. Separate the childhood fantasies, like being a fireman, (unless that was really a dream that you pursued) and write the dream about your future life that you may discover is the dream and destiny that God foreordained for you before the foundation of the world.

**MY DREAM:**

_____

_____

_____

_____

_____

_____

_____

_____

_____

_____

2. What did I do with that dream?

_____ Believe it.

_____ Ignore it.

_____ Pursue it.

3.  If I did not believe it, or I failed to pursue it, what should I now do with that dream?

_____

_____

_____

_____

_____

4.  If that childhood dream was for my life and I did not pursue it, but NOW I want to believe it and pursue it, what actions should I take?

ACTION ONE:

_____

ACTION TWO:

_____

ACTION THREE:

_____

5.  When was the destiny of your life written by God?

_____    At your birth?

_____    When you were conceived by your parents

_____    When God created the world?

_____    Before the creation of matter (the foundation
            of the world)?

If the dream that God placed in my life was really created and spoken into existence by God before the foundation of the world, I need to describe the value of and the importance that God would have me place on that dream.

6.  Put into words what you are going to do with the dream.

_____

_____

_____

_____

_____

_____

_____

7.  According to Revelation 17:8 and Hebrews 4:3, our names or our destiny and our works or accomplishments were written by God before the foundation of the world (before matter was created). Attempt to describe not only the importance of what God wrote, but also attempt to write a summary of God's word about you before He created the world. When you write your comments, remember that IF God wrote your destiny and created the dreams inside of you before He made a piece of matter, the words He wrote about you may be more important than creation itself.

(See chapter 20—"The Transcendence of the Dream.")

_____

_____

_____

_____

_____

_____

_____

# XXVI - HOW TO LIVE OUT OF A DREAM

_____

_____

_____

_____

_____

_____

_____

_____

_____

## NOTES

_____

_____

_____

_____

_____

_____

_____

_____

_____

_____

_____

_____

## Chapter 1

# THE MEETING

It seemed like another ordinary day. It was the nearly perfect summer. The weather had been beautiful, most of the days had been over 80 degrees. Often my mind went back to the years I had owned a beautiful cabin cruiser on the Niagara River and Lake Erie, and I thought how wonderful it would be if I still owned that boat in this perfectly beautiful weather. But those days were over. My world had changed. I was soon to celebrate my 80th birthday, and I could not have imagined how great life could be for a preacher in this season of his life.

As I drove into the parking lot outside the church office, I thought about the beautiful 40 acres that God had given our family--the horses, the farm animals, the beautiful little pond with its paddle boat and row boat. Then, my beautiful daughter who lived beside me with her wonderful husband and, of course, my two lovely granddaughters. Aimee and I had worked together in ministry for over twenty years. How much better and fulfilling could life be than this?

Today, I was about to meet one of my favorite people. I so looked forward to that visit. He was such a good friend, and had contributed so much of his talent to our life and ministry. I thought, both of us are busy, but I should just make time to sit down and talk like we are going to do today.

As I turned into the parking space, I looked at the car parked beside me. As my friends got out of the car, my heart kind of skipped a beat. As I looked into their faces, I wondered what was on their minds.

The three of us walked into the office and sat down at the little round table. They asked, "How are you?" I thought: that is a very appropriate question. In spite of all of the good things in life, it had been a hard year. I had fallen a year ago, resulting in the shattering of two major bones and two major surgeries that inserted two metal plates from the knee to the ankle with thirteen screws. My recovery process had been intense and difficult, with months in a wheelchair and on a walker. But, now, I was walking almost perfectly again, and the recovery of a person my age to full health was really a miracle. So the question about how I was doing was a normal one for close friends.

After I told them how well I was doing, immediately came the next statement, "Pastor, you need to resign as pastor and turn this church over to a successor, or in five years there will not be a church." Little did I know how that statement would change and impact my life for the positive. At first it was difficult to hear. I attempted to make my response positive.

Suddenly, a second question raced across my mind, "Maybe they are right, after all in a few months I will be eighty years old." But my mind argued, "I have a young pulpit pastoral staff, they provide young ideas for our church, and this congregation has the best of two worlds. The world of my maturity combined with my futurist mentality and the world of two strong young visionary preachers who work with me provides a very skilled and futuristic thinking team. Many new families comment about the effectiveness of this combination evident in our leadership team.

I immediately turned to the Holy Spirit and asked the question, "What are YOU saying to me through this meeting?"

My journey began. It was to be an exciting one as I asked myself a number of questions.

When I came to this church forty-nine years ago, I determined, at that time, I would give the rest of my life to lead this ministry. In fact, that was my vow before God--to give the rest of my life to this final chapter of ministry.

Today, although numerically I am older, "How can I resign my vow before God?" I walked over to the bathroom, looked in the mirror, and asked myself another penetrating question, "Is it time to finish my course and retire to Florida?"

That question had its interesting implications. Until a year ago, we had a home in Florida. My step-mother, Yolanda, had a lovely home on the waterfront of Clearwater Beach, and as she grew older, she needed the income we could provide to maintain this home. As I stood at the mirror the next morning, I realized that door was closed. Yolanda, had gone to be with the Lord last year and the home had just been sold. After forty years of having a second home in Florida, we no longer had a place to live there. That was no longer an option.

Then, as usual, I asked myself how I could turn this experience into a new dimension in God for my future. For days, I wrestled with myself. I did not want to resign or retire. In fact, I was very interested in turning the senior eldership to another person, but remain in what could be defined as a "Bishop's role", but this is not what the couple wanted me to do.

I prayed, "God, make what could have been a negative meeting into a gateway for a new dimension in my life." Suddenly, I heard this voice inside of me. It was that still, small voice, but it had an echo that seemed to be heard by the entire planet. The words came cascading over my whole being. The words engulfed me. The words challenged me, but still I did not know the answer to the question that was formed with the words. Like a heavenly airplane carrying a huge banner, I heard those words reverberate across the heavens. "How do you resign from something that is inside of your heart? I wondered and I prayed.

## THE DREAM WORKBOOK
## QUESTIONS FOR CHAPTER 1

When we have an encounter with a person or an event that seems to be negative, do you think that God may have a purpose for that event? In Chapter 1 of this book, Pastor Reid had an experience that at first seemed negative, but it became a bridge to the future of his life. Take a moment to describe an experience in your life that seemed to be negative, but later became a bridge to your future.

_____

_____

_____

_____

_____

_____

_____

_____

_____

Pastor Reid begins his description of the conflict between the world of dreams and vision inside of him and the seeming reality of the world around him. Have you experienced this conflict? Take a moment to describe this conflict between the vision and dream inside of you and the world around you.

_____

_____

_____

_____

_____

_____

_____

_____

_____

Is there a dream inside of you that could solve a problem in our world?  Describe the dream, the problem it would solve, and how it would bring change to the world.

_____

_____

_____

_____

_____

_____

_____

_____

_____

_____

_____

*Chapter 2*

# HOW DO YOU RESIGN SOMETHING THAT IS INSIDE OF YOU?

I knew instinctively that my friends had been sent into my office to give me a "word from God." Perhaps it was not the word they thought they were speaking, but I live on a different planet than most people. I hear things others do not hear. I walk in a cadence others do not join.

The words formed a question that seemed to have no answer, but gave me an insight as to what had gone on inside of me for decades. The words came like a freight train that would not stop, "HOW DO YOU RESIGN FROM A CHURCH THAT IS INSIDE OF YOU?" I had never thought of that before.

One night, forty-nine years ago, when I was first interviewed by the Board of the church I now pastor, I realized something very significant. As I sat with those wonderful men around the conference table, I realized they were not an employer hiring an employee. They were looking into the eyes of the person who had been chosen by God to come to Buffalo and pastor the church where they were Board members.

Both the Board of The Tabernacle and I faced one question: "Would we do what God had predestined for us to do with the future of this church?" I believed that my name (or destiny) was written by God before the foundation of the world. I was predestined by God to pastor this church even before God made the world.

As I sat at the table with those men that night, I looked around me. This was the world that had been inside of me ever since I was eight years old. I remembered the day in our little house in South Wales, NY as I lay in a bed, crippled by polio, unable to walk. My mother walked into the room, and I looked at her and said, "Will I ever walk again?"

She looked down at her son and said with real confidence in her voice, "Of course you will, BY JESUS' STRIPES YOU WERE HEALED." We both knew that I would walk again.

One morning I awakened early and heard what I now believe were the words of Jesus who said to me, "Tommy I am going to come and heal you today." I believed those words and called my mother to my bedside. I asked her to call the Pastor to come and pray for me. I told her that Jesus had spoken to me and if the Pastor came and prayed I would be healed. My mother called the Pastor. He was not available and could not come until the next day.

At first I was disappointed feeling that now I would not be healed. But suddenly, the same voice came again, "Tommy, the Pastor is not here, but I am Jesus. I am here, and if you take me by the hand, I will heal you." At that moment, something happened inside of me. With great difficulty, I pulled myself up from the bed, took my first step, then the second. I walked to the stairs and then began to run. I was healed!

That day, I learned two things. I learned to hear His voice and grasp his hand. It was the day when everything in life changed for me. It was not only a physical healing from being a cripple, but I learned how to hear His voice, to take His hand, and to let Him lead and guide me.

My life would be forever shaped by His Voice and His Hand. Never again would I make a decision without hearing His voice and grasping His hand as He led me through the decisions of life.

As I began to walk, the visions that God gave me about my life when I was laying on that bed came alive. I began to see a lifetime of ministry. I first saw myself preaching the Word of God in America in large healing evangelistic crusades. Then the vision changed, and I was standing among large crowds in other nations. People were getting out of wheelchairs and beds of affliction raising their hands and demonstrating to thousands of people the healing miracles of Jesus. Finally, after years of ministering to large crowds all over the world in healing meetings, I would come back home and build a church in Buffalo, NY.

When I sat in Buffalo being interviewed by the Board of The Tabernacle, I believe they saw a man with a vision and I saw men that were part of a vision that God had given me twenty-three years earlier.

I remembered what I saw in that vision. That church began to form inside of me. It continued to grow. It impacted an entire city and grew into many churches. It was not an ordinary church. It touched every part of a city. It ministered to the poorest in the city, the downtrodden in the city, and it reached into the homes and families of the rich and the well-known of the city. I would touch a city.

As I traveled across the world, that church inside of me began to grow. Sometimes it exploded within me. There were times when the work I was doing made me push the inner vision down, and I would concentrate on the success that was then happening around me. But the vision never went away.

When I went to the Philippines to pastor what was then the largest church in my denomination, the other church in my heart was overwhelmed with the thousands sitting in the church in the Philippines where I was the Pastor. I tried to push it down, reminding God how successful I was in Asia. Why would I ever return to my home city? After all, look at what I was doing now! But it would never go away.

As I sat with the Board that night in Buffalo, I realized I had not come here to work for someone or be hired by someone. I came here to build the church that was inside of my heart. It was then only a speck in the eye of God and a dream in the heart of God.

That is the reason that I could not resign to a board or a church that had not hired me. This was between Tommy Reid and God. Only He was capable of taking my resignation.

And beside all of that, the church I serve is not simply on the corner of Orchard Park Road and Southwestern Boulevard. This church was in my heart. And this morning as I looked at that couple on the other side of my desk telling me it was time to retire and resign as pastor, I asked the question, "To whom do I submit that resignation?" And where does the church in my heart go if I resign?

I thought to myself, that would be like Henry Ford resigning the headship of the Ford Motor Company, or Henry Kaiser resigning his company. He was the company...

Well, I was on a spiritual journey, and it would be an exciting one. Go with me on that journey.

## THE DREAM WORKBOOK
## QUESTIONS FOR CHAPTER 2

1.  When you read that Pastor Reid saw that the church he pastored was not only in a physical location, but, in reality, was in his heart and that he wondered how he could resign something in his heart, what did you see in your heart? Has it been created and planted in the world? If you planted that dream in the world, then describe what is in your heart.

_____

_____

_____

_____

_____

_____

2.  If there is a dream in your heart and, as yet, you have not experienced or created your dream, take a moment to describe the dream in your heart that you believe is your destiny or purpose in life.

_____

_____

_____

_____

_____

_____

## Chapter 3

# THE WORLD AROUND YOU
# AND
# THE WORLD INSIDE OF YOU

There are two worlds in which all of us live. There is the world around us and there is the world inside of us. They are two very different worlds. If we spend all of our time developing the world around us, we will never create the world inside of us. I have always faced this dilemma. It is so easy to live only in the world around us. It is so difficult to develop the world inside of us.

I was only 26 years of age when I was chosen as the Pastor of the largest church in my denomination located in Manila, Philippines. I felt like I was at the very highest point of success. As I stood in that significant pulpit I wondered why I should turn to the world inside of me, when the world around me was so very successful. Therefore, I would push that vision down where it would not disturb the world around me. After all, I could not live in both worlds.

Within two years, I would go to Korea and work with the man who would become the Pastor of the largest church in Christian history, Dr. Paul Cho. As I stood before the huge crowds in Korea, I constantly tried to dismiss the world inside of me.

One day, as I sat on a train in Korea with Dr. Cho, he turned to me and said, "Would you give me the rest of your life and be my co-pastor? We will together build the largest church in the world." You will never know how much I loved the Philippines and Korea. I was not enamored with the success I was enjoying, I was in love with the people, and I did not know how I could leave them.

But the vision of the church in Buffalo would not go away I even carried a copy of Aimee Semple McPherson's book, This Is That, containing the story of her building Angeles Temple, the largest church in her day. I asked myself, "Was her vision like the one that plagued me and kept coming to the surface in my heart?" I knew how she must have felt as she stood before large crowds in the eastern United States, while the church in Los Angeles that did not exist in the natural kept becoming the passion of her life.

Like Sister McPherson and myself, we all live in two worlds. There is the world around us. In this world we do the ordinary things of life: We get up in the morning, we eat breakfast, we go to work, we succeed in business or ministry, and we go to bed at night.

Satisfaction for our success floods our spirit, but the knowing of another world keeps a certain amount of dissatisfaction in our spirit. Every man and woman faces the same dilemma.

Mothers look at their three children, but know there is a dream inside for another child they have never met. Men and women with a successful business that is making millions of dollars, keep feeling a dissatisfaction that emerges when they feel another business inside of their heart.

Henry Ford felt like that many times in his life. Nothing ever satisfied him. When he made cars, he wanted to make glass, and so he formed a glass company. When he used other people's steel, he wanted to make his own. So he formed a steel company and made glass and steel.

Henry Kaiser felt the same way after he acquired his first business, built his first road, constructed his first dam, and built his first ship or his first automobile. There was always another business or another industry inside of him.

Ford, Kaiser, and every successful person lives in two worlds. There is a world of destiny and dreams inside of them, and there is a world of physical reality around them that is very different. Successful people always encounter the same passionate conflict between our two worlds. I have had the privilege of living in that amazing place in life where I have had to do the balancing act between the two worlds.

It has been a lifetime of juggling these two worlds. It is so easy, even for dreamers and visionaries, to retreat to the lesser world around them and forget the exciting world of Divine Destiny inside of them.

So, this is my story. It is my struggle. It is the story and struggle of every successful man or woman in the history of the world. Joseph lived in that struggle. So did Moses. So did every Prophet of God, and so did Jesus.

Let me help you define the struggle that is inside of you.

*Chapter 4*

# THE BATTLE BETWEEN THE WORLD AROUND YOU AND THE WORLD INSIDE OF YOU

I had been in Buffalo for over seven years. It was in that church where I met my wife. We married, and Wanda's talents greatly contributed to the ministry. One night, as Wanda I were lying in bed, the phone rang and something happened that could have detoured the entire vision. Up to this time, life had been a tremendous struggle for us.

I looked back at over seventeen years of ministry, and remembered that at twenty-six years of age, I was pastoring the largest church in our denomination. At twenty-nine years of age I was working with Dr. Cho in Korea and preaching to the largest crowds of my life. Then, at thirty-one, I had returned to the city where I knew God wanted to create the church that was in my heart. I was so excited. This was the city of my calling. This was the city of my dreams.

But my dream city did not bring the fulfillment of my dreams. Yes, we had a few successes. God had given us the gift of a beautiful piece of real estate through the generosity of my aunt, but the church just would not grow. I was discouraged, disillusioned, and feeling ready to quit.

Then, one day it happened. In the middle of this discouragement, God gave me three wonderful visitations of

His presence. Yet in spite of these visitations, the circumstances of the world around me were so very negative. The church that was inside of me was so different from the church that was around me. The church around me would not grow, yet the church inside of me was large and prosperous. The church around me had little if any influence in the city, yet the church inside of me was making a tremendous impact on the city.

In the midst of this conflict something happened that almost caused me to miss what God intended for my life. There was a secret desire inside of me that I had never told anyone, not even my wife. Although I knew that the church of my destiny and calling was in Buffalo, I retained the secret desire to pastor in Hawaii.

There was a church in Honolulu where I would minister each time I traveled back and forth to Asia. It was a church of over 1,000 people and every time I stood in that pulpit, it became the desire of my heart to be their Pastor. While I was in Honolulu I even went to a local television station to purchase time for a weekly telecast. There was always a conflict between where I wanted to pastor and where God had called me. I wanted to go to Honolulu, but God had destined me to go to Buffalo.

During those years I often argued with God. I told him that Buffalo was not working. It just would not grow. I told him how much I loved Honolulu and that perhaps I had made a mistake.

One night, in the midst of my discouragement, the phone rang. It awakened Wanda and myself in the middle of the night from a deep sleep. On the other end of the line a familiar voice said, "Tommy, you have just been elected as the new pastor of First Assembly in Honolulu." I could not believe it.

Things just were not working in Buffalo, and now the church and city of my soul-centered dreams was calling, and I was the newly elected pastor!

I began to wrestle with my heart, and with the call of God. Perhaps, this church inside of me that was in Buffalo, was not the right church for me. After all, the city where I really wanted to pastor, has just elected me. This must be the will of God.

But I had to wrestle with another question. The church in Honolulu was very real, and I loved it. It existed in the real world of today. It had over 1,000 people every Sunday. I had talked with a television station, and they had already agreed to sell us time. Maybe my vision was really for Honolulu, not for Buffalo.

It was necessary for me to go back and look inside myself to find out. For hours, the battle raged inside me. I went back into my dreams of over twenty years and thought maybe I had made the mistake, that it really must be the will of God for me to go to Honolulu. Suddenly, I discovered the battle between the vision and dream in my heart and the reality of the world around me.

My decision now had to be made. Which world would I live in? That telephone call revived some of my own dreams about pastoring a church in Honolulu, my favorite city. Everything about the world around me pointed to the fact that Wanda and I should board a plane for Hawaii and accept the call we had just received.

But there was another voice inside of me. It said, "Tommy, there is a church inside of you that is bigger, greater, and more influential than the church that has just called you to be their pastor. You must live in the church that is inside of you. You must believe your heart.

This is the conflict inside all of us who dream. Our future is in vision form inside our heart. It is as real before it becomes physical reality as it is when it finally comes to pass.

God reminded me: Expect the fulfillment of the dream. It is as real as the church you have seen with your physical eyes. You will make a decision to vote in favor of the church inside of you when you believe the dream.

The conflict in my heart was the conflict inside all of us. We tend to think that which we see as physical reality is greater than the reality of that which is simply a dream or an idea. This is the battle that every Biblical leader in history has faced.

## THE DREAM WORKBOOK
## QUESTIONS FOR CHAPTERS 3 and 4

1.  Every visionary or dreamer lives in two worlds. The first is the dream or destiny inside of them and the second is the world around them. If you are experiencing this dichotomy in life, take a moment to describe how you feel.

_____

_____

_____

_____

_____

_____

2.  You have read of Pastor Reid describing his successes at the age of 26 when he was the Pastor of the largest church in his denomination and at 30, was working with Dr. Cho in building what became the largest church in the world. Yet, neither of these accomplishments was the dream or destiny

inside of him. Every dreamer lives this life of struggle. What is your struggle?

_____  MY SUCCESS AT WHAT I AM DOING
_____  MY FAILURE AT WHAT I AM DOING
_____  THE SEEMING IMPOSSIBILITY OF MY DREAM

_____  _____


3.  You were designed by God to live in two worlds. Describe those two worlds.

The world AROUND me:

_____

_____


The world INSIDE of me:

_____

_____


4.  In a few words, try to describe the battle between your two worlds. The world inside of you and the world around you.

_____

_____

_____

_____

_____

_____

_____

_____

5.   How "big" is the world inside of God?

**Answer:**  Since the world inside of God contained the entire UNIVERSE, then the WORLD INSIDE OF GOD WAS BIGGER AND GREATER THAN THE ENTIRE UNIVERSE. If the world inside of you was created by God before He created the entire universe, then the world inside of you is GREATER THAN THE PHYSICAL UNIVERSE.

This is why the DESTINY AND DESTINATION of Moses was greater than the physical Red Sea.

6.   What must I do to begin living in the dream inside of me instead of just the world around me?

_____

_____

_____

_____

_____

_____

_____

_____

_____

_____

_____

_____

_____

## *Chapter 5*

# THE JOSEPH FACTOR

Joseph, the dreamer, lived exactly where I was living. The world inside of him was so different from the world around him. Joseph saw himself in his dreams in a great position of authority, even over his own family. But they saw him under their own authority. The Joseph factor is the Joseph battle. The battle between the world inside of him and the world around him.

Inside of him was a dream. In fact, many dreams. But where did they come from? By what process? Perhaps we can gain some insight into what is happening inside of us from the life of Joseph.

The Bible says it this way: JOSEPH DREAMED A DREAM! It doesn't say what he ate for dinner. It doesn't say if his mother in their conversation had put any kind of idea in his head. It simply says, "Joseph dreamed a dream." I love that Biblical statement because that is the way it happens.

First of all, "Joseph dreamed." I think every person is a Joseph. Every one of his brothers must have had their own dreams. If Joseph did, they did. There is a little bit of Joseph in every man. There is a dreamer in everyone that has been born.

The difference among men is whether or not they arise in the morning and remember and believe the dream. The difference between people is not a division between dreamers and non-dreamers. The difference is remembering and believing. Some of us simply do not want to deal with the conflict between the world God gives us as a dream for our future and the reality of the world around us. It is just simply easier to live in the world around us.

Part of this conflict is whether or not we believe. Think about the people who created the automobile industry. Did you ever think of the conflict between the world around them and the world inside of them?

Inside of them they saw a world where there were automobiles, roads for them to drive on, gas stations for them to refuel and parking places for them to park. However, when they looked outside their doors, they saw no roads for cars to drive on, no gas stations to refuel, and there no parking places for them to park. Talk about a conflict between two worlds; everything around them said, "give up your dream, it doesn't fit into the world around you."

Understand this: if your dreams are God's dreams, they will never find a world that is big enough for them to fit.

David's world did not have room for a king who was a simple shepherd and played a harp and had no formal education. David's dream was really kind of crass. It just did not fit into the world around him. But then, remember, dreams come from another world.

We live in time. Dreams are born in eternity. We live in space. Dreams are born in the mind of God, not in the limitation of his created physical universe. In fact, that is probably one of our problems. We keep trying to fit our dreams into the physical universe that God created, but dreams by their very nature are not physical, they are much greater. They are part of the "unknown factor" that the Bible talks about when it says, "everything that we see was created from what we do not see."

God was not anxious when he gave Henry Ford the idea

to "put America on wheels." He had no problems with the fact that there were no roads, no gas stations, and no parking places. God's ideas are never contingent upon physical circumstances or physical limitations. They come from an eternal intelligence that created the heavens and the earth from nothing through the very essence of the dreams in His heart.

Which brings me to a question. Think about it. Just how much power is there in a dream? It is obvious that there is unlimited power in a dream. Just ask Joseph. For Joseph it was power over the murderous plot of his brothers who threw him into a well. It was power over the slave traders who found him in the desert. It was power over the inhuman treatment given him as he stood naked in the auction of a slave market. It was power over a life-time prison sentence. There is no limitation to the power of a dream.

That is why there is such a great conflict between our two worlds. The world inside of us is born in the limitless world of the unseen. The world around us is always limited by what we can see with our natural eyes. The world inside of us is born in the mind of a Creator who spoke the universe into existence. The world around us is controlled by the worries of a human race that spends a lifetime in negative thoughts.

No wonder the two worlds are on a collision course. They simply cannot coexist. The world inside of us is made to conquer the world around us. Just ask Joseph! Ask David! Ask Moses! Ask Jesus! Ask the blind man who cried out, "Jesus have mercy on me!"

There is something in all of us that is greater than any problem, greater than any sickness, greater than any limitation.

Look inside yourself for a moment. When you awaken, remember the words the Bible speaks about Joseph, "Joseph dreamed a dream." But remember, he did not only dream, he remembered. He spoke to others about it. He believed the dream!

## THE DREAM WORKBOOK
## QUESTIONS FOR CHAPTER 5

1.  Is the power of your dream greater than the power of the world around you? Think of Joseph's dream: Was it greater than the opposition of his brothers, the slave market, or his unfair imprisonment in Egypt? How big is the dream in your heart? Is it bigger and more powerful than the opposition of the world around you? If God had a whole universe in His heart, how big is the universe of the dream inside of you?

_____

_____  _____

_____

_____

2.  Do you have the faith, or can you reach out to embrace a faith that sees a limitless world inside of you where anything that God dreams through you is possible? Describe how it would feel if you became that kind of person of faith and lived in a world without limits. In answering this question, think about how you would feel if you lived from a heart where there were no limits.

_____

_____

_____

_____

_____

*Chapter 6*

# GOD HAD A UNIVERSE IN HIS HEART

How big is God? All I know is that He is bigger than the entire universe, because everything in the universe was first of all in the heart of God. The universe was so small to God that it fit inside His heart. He spoke what He had in His heart and it became. The earth, the mountains, the seas, the sun, the moon, the stars, the constellations. In fact, everything that exists was first of all in God's heart and God's dreams.

Dreamers amaze me. Not because it is uncommon to dream, but because of how much God can literally press down, shake together, and put into a human heart the form of a dream. I am amazed when I read the story of one of my favorite dreamers, Henry Kaiser.

He dreamed roads and created them. He dreamed about the Golden Gate bridge and helped create it. He dreamed of the largest dam in the world and created it. He dreamed of building huge ocean-going ships on an assembly line, and he did it. The president of the United States told him we would lose World War II if we couldn't discover how to build hundreds of ocean-going freight ships in a very limited period of time. He said these ships must carry men, supplies, and weapons to battlefields across the world. Henry Kaiser dreamed of how to do it. Then, he did it!

The world is full of problems today because dreamers do not

dream. If all of the people into whom God places His dreams would dream and believe them, every problem in our world would be solved. Our problem is that we refuse to believe the dream that God has placed inside of us.

GOD HAD A UNIVERSE IN HIS HEART! How big is the heart of God? -- as big as all of the universe. Did you ever ask God, "How big is the human heart?"

Every building is a dream that God placed in the heart of a designer. Every city is a dream that God placed in the heart of a man. Every factory is a dream that God has placed in the heart of a human being. Your problem and mine is that we just don't realize the size of our heart. If God's heart was the dwelling place of an entire universe, think of how much God places in your heart.

A prophet came to the house of Jesse. God was looking for a man whose heart was big enough to contain an entire nation. Jesse brought every one of his sons before the prophet. Each one was a talented, handsome young man. Every one looked like he could be a king. But, every son was rejected by God and therefore, by the prophet....that was, until a boy came from the field who lived under the open canopy of heaven and lived with sheep.

This son was very different from his brothers who lived in the confines of a house, David lived under the stars of the heaven. His view was limitless. Like Abraham, I believe he counted the stars at night. I believe he rose up early to watch the sun rise. He was stronger than lions or bears because of the man he knew was inside of him. He lived in a limitless world. When the prophet saw him, he saw the bigness of his heart and what it could contain. He said to himself, "Here is one after God's heart, here is one who thinks God's thoughts and dreams God's dreams." The prophet had never read one of David's songs or heard him play his harp. All he knew was that he looked beyond the suntanned skin and saw a heart big enough to contain God's dreams.

There is a universe prepared for your heart. It is already in the mind and heart of God, and it is intended for you. Are you willing to wake up tomorrow morning and remember the dream? Are you willing to risk the ridicule and the taunts of those who hear your dream and do not believe? It is risky. It is very humiliating. But when the dream in your heart is bigger than the humiliation of the disbelief of those who will not believe you, then God has a person He can use and trust with His dreams.

There is a universe that God wants to place in your heart, if you will believe.

*Chapter 7*

# A Dream
# The Size Of A Seed

When God created His universe He did something amazing. He placed in it something amazing that we call seeds. Every tree had a seed to recreate a new generation of trees. Every tomato was loaded with seeds. Every apple had seeds. Every animal had seeds. In fact, everything in creation had the power to re-create itself through a seed.

Dreams are seeds. When God talked about the miracle of resurrection He said, "When you plant a seed, it does not resemble the plant that is inside of it any more than the body you plant in death resembles the resurrection body."

That is the truth about dreams. Dreams by their very nature are only seeds, not fully developed. By their nature, for seeds to produce they must grow. To understand the power of a dream you must understand the power of a seed.

Let me take a moment to describe to you what it is like to have a seed dream in your heart. We have talked about the size of the human heart, but for a moment let's talk about the size of the seed that God places in that heart.

How did it feel when a small boy, about twelve years of age, walked to the altar of a little Pentecostal church and God placed a dream in his heart? To further complicate the problem, he was sickly. In fact he was crippled, and he stutters, unable to barely get a full sentence out of his mouth. He is very shy and embarrassed to be around people. There is nothing that qualifies him to be a man with a vision.

But God is not limited by human inadequacies. God is looking for dreamers. God is looking for a man or woman who will wake up in the morning and say like Joseph did, "World, I had a dream."

I was that boy, and at that altar in a little church on Elm Street in East Aurora, NY, God planted a dream. But that dream was only a seed that I was responsible to plant to see God do the miracle of growth. Let me tell you the story of the growth of a seed.

It was then just a seed. Yet, I knew that the little seed in my heart was very important, for it had the potential to grow into something very large and significant. But I lived in a very small world. Something inside of me was alive. I felt it move. Every day it changed. Every day, it grew. Every day, I discovered something different about that little seed in my heart.

I began to discover some things about that seed as it grew and changed inside of me. In it, there was a preacher. You see, the seed inside of me was very different from the world around me. In the physical world, I was a stutterer. When the teacher would ask me to give a report, the words just would not come out. Children would laugh because the little boy with the seed of a preacher could not speak.

I had to learn at the age of eight the difference between my two worlds. Which world would I believe? In the world inside of me I was standing before large crowds and eloquently preaching the Gospel of Jesus Christ, but in the physical world around me I could not express a fully developed sentence. At eight, with the help of a believing mother, I decided to believe in the greater world inside of me.

As Bishop Knox so eloquently stated in the Foreward of this book, I felt like the disciples who were with Jesus on the boat in the midst of a storm that could have meant the end of their physical lives. Even as fishermen, they were afraid. But in the back of the little ship was their friend, Jesus, who was peacefully sleeping! I look at that scene and realize that there was a difference between what was inside of Jesus and what was inside of the disciples. Jesus had peace inside of him. The disciples had the experience of seeing storms that took people's lives. They believed in the world around them. Jesus believed that the peace inside of Him was greater than the storm that was around Him. That was the difference between Jesus and the disciples. They understood the power of the storm in the world around them. Jesus believed in the power of the peace inside of Him.

I had to learn that lesson early in life. There was something inside of me that was greater than the world around me, for inside of me was a preacher.

As I think about those years, I recall other conflicts. My parents and I went to the only Pentecostal church in our community.   It was very small with fewer than fifty adult members. It was my world. Dad was a deacon and led the worship. My mother was a Sunday school teacher and had more people in her Saturday children's program than there were people at church on Sunday!

In my heart there was greatness and largeness. I saw myself preaching to large crowds, pastoring very large churches, affecting whole cities, building ministries around the world, but the only world I knew was small and unknown to the rest of the world. Which world would I live in?

By the age of ten, I had decided to live in the world inside of me. The world around me was small, the world inside of me was very large, very exciting, and more effective. In the world around me, my beloved pastor was disloyal to his wife. I decided to live a life that had great integrity. In the world around me there was lack, but in the world inside of me there was the provision of God. I decided that I must make that critical choice, and I would choose the world inside of me.

But as my thinking progressed, and I realized that my inside world did not exist in physical reality, the seed inside of me was growing. I had to face the fact that there was a physical world of reality. I must not become a person who just lived in a dream world.

At the same time the seed inside of me grew in vision, the world around me did not seem to change. The church was still small. In the world around me I saw leaders who lacked integrity. In the world that was growing inside of me, I knew I needed to be a man of great integrity.

I came to realize I must let the God who lived inside of me create a larger world like the world that lived inside of me.

To do what I dreamed of doing with my life, I must enter a world of growth. Nothing, I discovered, would be delivered instantly. It must begin as a seed of vision, and I must grow into that vision. Being young, I realized this would require time and preparation.

It would be fifty or sixty years before everything that was inside of me became a reality in our world. I had to give it time to grow, and prepare myself for that growth.

And that is the wonderful miracle of the seed. It grows. And, something amazing was growing inside of me.

*Chapter 8*

# THE SEED GROWS

I am so grateful to God that I was very young when God placed these dreams in my heart. I did not attempt to be a boy preacher at eight. I was just simply a little boy. I played with cars. I loved to play and pretend and enjoy a dream world with my young friends. As I wrestled with the world outside of me being so different from the world inside of me, I did not try to create that world immediately. I simply let the seed grow.

My first decision was to spend time with God. Sunday was very special to me, especially Sunday night. I listened to every word of my Sunday school teachers. I remember my teachers in the small church in East Aurora, and I remember especially my teacher at Central Assembly of God in Springfield, MO, Mrs. Lawrence. Her husband was a leading businessman in that city, and she became the person in my life whom I could emulate.

I also remember the services in church, the great revival meetings in the Shrine Mosque with thousands of people. I remember being prayed for to receive a new anointing of the Holy Spirit by Evangelist Lorne Fox, and the remarkable change that took place in my life as I lay in the sawdust in that huge tent after he laid hands on me.

Life became a spiritual journey. As I grew and progressed through the journey as a little boy in church, I had the world of vision that God had placed in my heart. But through that journey, like other children around me, I simply let my church and all of its spiritual mentoring become my guiding light.

There were special times when the seeds inside of me had great growth. The first dramatic growth of a seed came through the inspiration of my best friend, Paul Crouch, who later founded the TBN network.

One day, Paul said to me, as he held a baseball in his hand, "Let's go and play catch." I tried not to hear. You see, my Dad was a professional athlete in both boxing and football. Obviously, I did not seem to inherit his athletic abilities. My major problem was in my eyesight and perception. I saw the ball in a different position than it was. I just could not coordinate my eyes with the ball coming toward me. Paul said, "Tommy, I'll teach you how to catch a ball."

He slowed me down in my thinking enough so I could see the ball, and put my hands where the ball was. By the end of the next couple of hours, I could catch a ball! Paul, who was also only about ten years of age, said, "Tommy, you can do anything you want to do." And I believed him. I often wonder who I would be if it were not for that special day with the young Paul Crouch. No wonder my friend Paul created the largest television network in the world!

We must begin this journey with faith. Faith becomes activated as we discover that we must "grow" into the vision inside of us. It will never happen overnight. We must remember the dream is simply a seed, and the seed must have time to grow.

As I remember that incident so many decades ago, I have one regret. I wish I had let that ball catching seed grow within me. I still do not catch well. I wonder what would have happened if I had let the seed grow through practice and devoting myself to growing the seed. When you discover a seed, let it grow.

But there was a much mightier seed inside of me. That

was the seed of a church in Buffalo, and I had to let it grow. I decided to water and cultivate it until it became my very life. I let God develop it through prayer, hard work, education, and most of all through the growth of my faith.

Seeds by their very nature grow when they are planted in fertile soil. There is fertile soil in every heart, or God would not plant the seeds of His dreams there. Our job is to fertilize those seeds through believing in them, confessing them, and preparing our lives to fulfill them.

## THE DREAM WORKBOOK
## QUESTIONS ON CHAPTERS 6, 7, and 8

The dream inside of you is the size of a SEED. The seed has the natural ability to GROW into the dream or destiny that God has intended . We must therefore enter the world of GROWTH. SOMETHING AMAZING IS GROWING INSIDE OF YOU! In a few words, describe it.

_____

_____

_____

_____

_____

_____

_____

2. If my dream is a seed and a small seed grows into a mighty oak, then how limitless is the seed inside of me? When you think about the power of a seed and realize that

although your dream is the size of a seed, it has the limitless power of a seed, describe how that makes you feel.

_____

_____

_____

_____

_____

_____

_____

_____

_____

_____

3.   Am I permitting the seed of destiny, purpose and vision inside of me to grow, or am I, by my own attitudes and lack of faith, "killing" that seed?

_____

_____

_____

_____

_____

_____

_____

_____

_____

_____

_____

## Chapter 9

# FAITH TO TEST THE SEED

The test of a vision is always provision. Every dream, every vision, even our destiny itself must be tested. No matter how much you believe in something that is inside of you, there comes a time when that dream or vision must be tested, endure the test, and qualify as divine. Of course, you cannot do that immediately, as the the test would come back negative. However, after you have sowed your seeds of prayer and preparation into the vision, you must put the vision to its greatest test. That test is the provision of God.

Bobbie Schuller, the grandson of the famed Robert Schuller, tells the story of going to his grandfather as a teenager and telling "Grandpa," as he calls him, about the call of God on his life to take a short-term missions trip that would cost several thousand dollars. A teenager, young Robert did not have the funds for his dream. So, he went fishing with "Grandpa."

While they were relaxing in the little fishing boat, he told his Grandfather about his dream of a missions trip and the cost. He said he expected that Grandpa, who then was raising millions of dollars for world evangelism, would probably offer some monetary help. He thought, surely, the great man of faith would be the first donor to his missions project.

Instead, Robert Schuller looked at his grandson and said, "If God has spoken to your heart and called you to go, then God will provide the funds." Now in his thirties and at this writing this preaching Pastor, who now fills his grandfather's pulpit, says, "That was the greatest lesson my grandfather could have taught me."

You see, our grandfathers of the faith are not our provision. The combination of a God-implanted vision and faith in the God of provision is our source. But we must come to the time when we test the source. How does that work?

What makes the seed that is within us work? All of us as individuals have remarkable seeds of vision and destiny within us. However, only a minority of the people of the earth activate these seeds with faith. Therefore, most of these extremely valuable seeds are never utilized and never bear fruit. There are millions of books that have never been written; millions of great songs that lie dormant in the human heart and have never been composed. There are huge business empires larger than the empire built by Andrew Carnegie or Henry Ford that are buried in a human heart and have never been built.

What is the difference between the two seeds? One seed is sown in a believing heart, the other in the heart of one who does not believe. When I was wrestling with whether or not to believe the dreams and visions that were inside of me, and attempting to find out if they were really my destiny or only an ego-driven pipe dream, I had an opportunity to test the dream locked inside of me. Was I really hearing the voice of God?

By this time, I had finished my formal education and had invested everything I had in getting myself ready to begin to live in the dream. The seed inside of me was going to be plunged into the world of destiny around me.

You see, I have always believed that the real test of a dream was whether or not there was divine provision for the fulfillment of the dream.

I would suggest to any person who has an unbelievable dream to test it honestly. I tested mine, and discovered the ability to believe for the rest of the dream.

Let me share with you the test that I used. I was in my last year of Bible College and in the final stages of launching out into the first dream that God had given me when I was a child. That first chapter of my vision was to become an evangelist who would preach large city wide-crusades.

My major problem was that not only did I not have any invitations to conduct crusades, but I had no transportation. So, I decided to test both my faith and my calling. The invitations were not my responsibility, but believing for the finances to travel from church to church was my personal responsibility. I had no funds to provide, so I had to believe for the funds. Robert Schuller was right, "If the vision is from God, He will make full provision for the work He has called you to do."

So, allow me to share with you what I did. I worked as hard as I could. I saved every penny I could save. I did everything in my own power to find the funds to purchase the vehicle to drive throughout America. The rest was up to God. I would believe; He would provide. So I prayed. That was a great idea. It is not just one option among many. It is our only option.

When I prayed, I felt the Lord saying to me that I was to be very specific to name the exact vehicle I both needed and desired. I was carrying a Hammond organ with a Leslie tone cabinet to all of our scheduled meetings. Therefore, I needed a vehicle that could carry the organ. Although as a graduating college student I had absolutely no funds, I went to many showrooms and shopped. I decided that the best vehicle for my use was a new Pontiac sedan.

The year was 1952, just a few years after World War II, and vehicles were still scarce. I visited the Pontiac showroom, shared with the salesperson the vehicle that I needed. He said if I ordered the vehicle it would be more than a year in delivery.

Undaunted, I asked him for a brochure of the 1952 model year. He gave me one and I placed it in my Bible. I still have that brochure today. Every time I prayed, I took out the brochure and placed it before God, looked at the vehicle, and envisioned it to be mine. I told the Lord that it was to be black, with an 8-cylinder engine, manual or stick shift, and red wheels with wide whitewall tires. Every day, I prayed into the very specifics of that dream with the picture in front of me.

So I began to believe for the money. Things began to happen. A friend of ours in Kansas City sent my Dad a truck-load of fire extinguishers that were covered with mud from the great Kansas City flood. Our friend said to my Dad, "Sell them and get that car for Tommy." We cleaned off the mud and sold them for almost $1,000. Another man came into my Dad's office and left another large check. Now I thought that I had almost enough money to buy the vehicle, if I could only find a vehicle to buy.

One day after we had "believed in" a specific amount of money, my Dad, who was a great man of faith, said, "Tommy, it is time to get your car." I said to him, "But Dad, there are no cars available, and I told God that I wanted a 1952 black Pontiac sedan." My Dad said, "Let me make one telephone call."

He picked up the phone and called a Mr. Jarvis who was a Pontiac dealer in Sikeston, Missouri. Mr. Jarvis answered the phone and my Dad said, "Mr. Jarvis, we need a black Pontiac sedan delivery, do you have one?" Mr. Jarvis took a long pause, then said, "Al, you will not believe this, but a year ago a man came in and ordered a new black Pontiac sedan delivery with an 8-cylinder engine, wide whitewalls, red wheels and a standard transmission, and he just called me and said he did not want the vehicle. It is sitting here in the showroom."

My Dad said, "How much?" and Mr. Jarvis told him the exact amount that had been given to us for the vehicle!

Can you believe that this vehicle, to the exact detail of my faith confession, was ordered by this man one year before and was in the show room at exactly the time my Dad made the phone call.

As I drove away in that miracle vehicle, God began to make me aware that I had tested the call with my specific prayer. He let me know that this very miracle would confirm the call of God during difficult times. I have remembered this amazing incident many times, and every time it has confirmed the validity of my call.

I also believe that this prayer was a "test" of my calling. If God would miraculously provide a vehicle for this ministry, and the exact vehicle I had confessed to the Lord, then I would put God to the test. Every time I prayed that prayer for this vehicle, I was saying to the Lord, "This is a test, and if You have really called me then I know You will provide every need for this ministry the rest of my life." And He has.

The seed inside of us can be tested. Prayer for provision for the dream is our responsibility, while God's responsibility is the provision. Our dream always must be bigger and greater than our own ability. The vision always comes from the unseen world, and the provision for it is always beyond our capability.

God is the very life behind the seed, and He will confirm His call and vision through amazing provision, as it is the test of the call.

## THE DREAM WORKBOOK
## QUESTIONS ON CHAPTER 9

1.  Your TEST seed is the TEST OF PROVISION! Ask yourself the question, "Am I willing to 'wait' for the provision?" Also ask yourself how committed you are personally to the waiting period. Remember that Abraham did not wait, but took upon himself an action of making himself the provision. Take a few moments to reflect if you are really committed to faith in God's provision or will you either give up the dream or depend upon yourself. Write your commitment down in words.

_____

_____

_____

_____

_____

_____

_____

_____

_____

_____

_____

_____

_____

_____

2.    Pastor Reid tells in this chapter how he asked God for a specific car, in a specific color, with specific equipment. God gave him an absolutely phenomenal miracle that provided the exact car. How important is it for us to be exact in our requests to God for provision?

_____

_____

_____

_____

_____

_____

_____

_____

_____

3.    Identify the provision you need to fulfill the dream that is inside of you.

_____

_____

_____

_____

_____

_____

_____

_____

_____

## *Chapter 10*

# TEMPORARY SUCCESS IS NOT THE FULLY DEVELOPED SEED

S uccess, even great success, does not necessarily mean that the dreamer or visionary has reached the vision or dream that God has placed within him or her. You can literally be detoured from God's perfect plan for your life by believing that your present success is your destiny.

I began my ministry with great success. At 26, I was the pastor of the largest church in our denomination, following the world-renowned Dr. Lester Sumrall as his successor in the great church in Manila. We enjoyed an attendance of nearly 6,000 every Sunday. As I stood in that world pulpit, I could not believe where God had placed me. But my present success was not the seed God had placed inside of me. It was a step in the direction of my destiny, but it was not my destiny. The seed and dream inside of me was not fully-developed, and whatever success I had obtained was not its full manifestation.

After success in Manila, I came home to preach very successful city-wide crusades in America. Then came another telephone call from the Mission Department of the Assemblies of God and missionary John Hurston in Korea. They said there was a very promising young Korean man and asked if we would go to Korea.

Accepting their invitation, we went to Seoul in 1962 to work with a then unknown young man by the name of Paul Cho. The church Pastor Cho was leading was already experiencing great growth, and by the time we arrived already had over 300 members. During the next year of working together, we saw over 2,500 more added to Sunday attendance. Once again, I was experiencing success.

One day traveling with Pastor Cho on a train between Seoul and Taejon, he turned to me and said, "Tommy, I need you. Would you give me the rest of your life and become the co-pastor of the church in Seoul." I knew this church would have amazing growth, and I loved Korea. I did not know, however, that it would become the largest church in the history of the world. I wanted to accept his invitation to stay and partner with him.

At the same time, the seed for building churches in Buffalo was growing inside of me. I knew that it was not yet fully developed, but inside of me I wanted to return to Buffalo, the city of my calling, no matter how successful I was at that moment.

I turned to the man who would become Dr. David Cho and said, "I cannot stay in Korea with you, it is not my calling. I love you, and I love Korea, but my calling is Buffalo. I must go back to my calling."

It would have been very easy for me to confuse successes in the Philippines and Korea as the fulfillment of the vision or church inside of me, but I knew that the large church in Manila and the growing success of the church in Korea were not the church that was in my dreams.

I had a lot of growing to do. I had lot of confusing experiences to go through, and had much discouragement yet to pass through. Something inside of me told me that no matter how successful my life was on the outside, it was not the fulfillment of the destiny that was inside of me.

In those moments I turned to what I felt in my heart. I had to discover the wonder of what God had placed there and believe that it would happen.

## THE DREAM WORKBOOK
## QUESTIONS ON CHAPTER 10

## Temporary SUCCESS does not indicate a FULLY- DEVELOPED SEED.

1.  I must take a very definitive look at my life and ask myself several questions:
    (Circle the right answer)

    a.  Am I a success in my life today?
        _____ Yes
        _____ No

    b.  Am I doing today what God's dreams are for me?
        _____ Yes
        _____ No

    c.  Is my success the enemy of my destiny?
        _____ Yes
        _____ No

    d.  Is my failure the enemy of my destiny?
        _____ Yes
        _____ No

e. This is the list of changes in life that I need to make to fulfill my destiny.

_____

_____

_____

_____

_____

_____

_____

_____

_____

2. Do I need to DISCOVER THE WONDER OF WHAT IS INSIDE OF ME? Or, do I know what is there and have I lost my faith? If so, describe the feelings inside of you.

_____

_____

_____

_____

_____

_____

_____

_____

_____

_____

## Chapter 11

# THE SEED IS SUPERNATURAL

### The supernatural seed is supernatural: The story of The Tabernacle

We must always be aware that seed is supernatural. We think if we just get enough education, if we work hard enough, if we develop the best of our talents, we can create the dream. Jesus did not say that. He said, "I will build My church," not that we would build it. Seed is supernatural and is not the result of great human talent or ego-based dreams to be bigger and greater than the other person.

After we had experienced a great outpouring of the Holy Spirit in Buffalo, we had amazing growth in our church. According to some statistics our church grew until we had the largest Sunday attendance of any church in the northeastern United States.

I knew that I was not the central figure or the reason for that growth. I must never take the credit. This was easy for me, because it was very obvious in our case that the growth of the church that was inside of me was not a result of my own talents or my own efforts.

When we have great success in our lives, and see the dream inside of us fulfilled, we must realize that our success is not the result of our own ego-driven desire for riches or greatness. True dreams are given to us by God and have a divine connection. They are directly connected to the universal plans of God for His world.

Joseph's dream was directly connected with the purposes of God for the nation of Israel and the birth of a Messiah. Moses' dream to lead God's people to escape imprisonment was not simply because he loved his people, but it had a direct connection to the purposes of God to bring the family who would give birth to the Messiah to the land where the prophets prophesied He would be born. Saul's burning passion for truth was not just a religious obsession with organized religion. It was directly related to the dream in his heart to discover God. That passion resulted in a dramatic encounter with the living Christ on the road to Damascus. That encounter led the converted Saul to become a man who would change his world for Christ. All of these men were born with the dream of God in their hearts.

And so it was with the dream of destiny in my heart. I was born at a specific time in history when all of the elements of God's purposes were brought into connection in my own life. I thought this dream to build a large church in Buffalo, NY was just about church growth, and I would build a church of a thousand people. But God had far different plans. I was to have a divine encounter with history.

First, I had three divine encounters with God that would prepare me for my appointment with history and divine destiny. God said, almost with an audible voice, "Never again ask Me to anoint what you are doing, but become part of what I am doing." And I made an amazing discovery: God was doing something dramatic on His earth. My life had been brought into existence to literally collide with God's activities on the earth.

I had been thinking and planning how to build a great church. Instead, God sovereignly decided to pour out His

Spirit in the Roman Catholic parish down the street from the little church where I was the pastor. I thought God had put a large church inside of my heart for me to build. God had bigger plans, and His purpose for me was to simply "fit" into the things He was doing on the earth.

At the same time, God was even doing other things on the earth on the campuses of high schools, colleges and universities. The Jesus movement was happening, and thousands of young people were coming to Christ.

These two movements were to converge on the little piece of property where our church stood. When my world and God's world converged with each other, suddenly we had a large church. The church in my heart was literally created in a period of three or four weeks as Catholic Charismatics and the Jesus people made their way into the building where I was preaching.

And that is my point--the seed of God is supernatural. God does not need our abilities, our talents, or our education to accomplish His purposes for us. The true purposes of God that have filled our heart with His destiny require not just our talents, but a convergence with God's plans.

That has always been true. Joseph's dreams were not the product of an ego-driven boy who wanted to be greater than his brothers. His dreams were directly related to Godly purposes for the people of God, the nation in Egypt, and the future history of the world.

You see, the real dreams and visions authored by God are attached to history. Therefore, they are not a product of our ego; they are part of history that God is writing for the universal creation. You are a part of history. Your life is directly related to the sovereign purposes of God for the world and for humanity.

The dreams that God has placed in your heart have to do with the purposes and plans of God for the earth. You are a part of history. When we find God, we find out where we fit into His plans for divine destiny for His world.

## THE DREAM WORKBOOK
## QUESTIONS ON CHAPTER 11

1.  The seed is SUPERNATURAL. In writing, make a definitive declaration that you believe the seed is divine and is supernatural.

_____

_____

_____

_____

_____

_____

_____

2.   Our divinely-inspired dreams are authored by GOD! Make a declaration that the dreams inside of you are divine, are of supernatural origin and, therefore, need supernatural provision. Declare it in words.

_____

_____

_____

_____

_____

_____

3.   Truly God inspired dreams have to do with the PURPOSE OF THE GOD ON THE EARTH.  How do your dreams "fit" into the purposes of God on the earth to bring healing to people, change to culture and society, and make a difference for God according to His plan and purpose and not yours? Make a statement in writing about the connection of your dreams to the purposes of God.

_____

_____

_____

_____

_____

_____

_____

_____

_____

_____

_____

_____

4.     If I fulfill God's dream for my life, will I be a part of HISTORY? Try to imagine yourself in a history book on the time in which you live.  Write a short sentence or two about how you have brought the manifestation of the Kingdom of God to earth and have fulfilled His will through your success. Make a declaration that the dream is not about your success but about God's will and purposes..

MY STATEMENT:    I am a part of history.  I have spent my life fulfilling the purposes of God on the earth.

My story in being part of God's plan is....

_____

_____

_____

_____

_____

_____

_____

_____

_____

_____

_____

_____

_____

_____

_____

_____

_____

_____

_____

# SECTION 2

# DREAMERS IN HISTORY

## Chapter 12

# HENRY KAISER

## (THE DREAMER)

There are many men in history who have captured my imagination. No man does it in a greater way than the famed Henry Kaiser. We know him for Kaiser Steel, Kaiser Cement, Kaiser-Frazer automobiles and a score of other great business adventures. Let's take a quick look at his life. No life in the history of the world demonstrates the conflict between the world inside of us and the world around us as does his..

Henry Kaiser was born in a little town called Sprout Brook, near Utica, NY in 1882. From the very beginning he demonstrated an understanding for the next great trend in the world. In the early 1900's, he developed an interest in the field of photography. He went to Lake Placid, NY and offered to work for nothing at a local camera store. He obtained an agreement with the owner, whose store was failing, that if he doubled sales in a year, he would become a partner in the business. Henry Kaiser tripled the sales! Now, owning a large percentage of the business, the store's former owner and now partner, felt unable to keep up with Kaiser, and offered to sell him the entire business.

In 1905, he married Bess Fosburgh. In 1907, the couple moved to Spokane, Washington. There, he talked his way into a salesman's job at a hardware store. While working at the store, he became acquainted with many contractors and became interested in the construction business. In 1909, he went to work for a cement and gravel company, and gained a great deal of experience in the construction. On December 14, 1914, he formed the Henry J. Kaiser Company, Ltd. in Vancouver, British Columbia. Seeing the emergence of the transportation in the world, Kaiser decided to focus on building much-needed roads. He built roads throughout the United States and Canada. Kaiser worked from a large tent that was moved from job to job. He was tough and relentless. His emphasis was always on speed and getting the job done immediately so he gained the nick-name "Hurry Up Henry."

In 1927, Kaiser negotiated his first major contract in the nation of Cuba. There, he built over 200 miles of roads in a huge twenty million dollar project. Overcoming many difficulties, he did the unthinkable and finished the project a year ahead of schedule. Henry Kaiser was off and running.

He then turned to an even bigger task, the Hoover Dam. The project was so large that the government decided to use more than just one contractor. So Kaiser teamed up with W.A. Bechtel Corporation, and became part of a larger consortium known as Six Companies, Inc. It was the largest dam built up to that time and was completed two years ahead of schedule. Later Kaiser worked on the Booneville Dam and the San Francisco Bay Bridge.

My favorite Henry Kaiser story is the building of the Liberty and Victory ships that made it possible for us to win World War II. Unable to get supplies to both Asia in our conflict with Japan and to Europe in our conflict with the armies of Germany and Italy, we were destined to lose the war to those who would have taken over the whole world. It is said that Franklin Delano Roosevelt called the famed builder into his office and informed him that if someone could not build ships faster, we would lose the war. Kaiser told the President that he built dams, bridges, and roads, but he had never built ships. But by the end of their conversation, Kaiser declared: "If it can't be done, then I will do it."

To this day there are two things in my office that inspire me. One is this statement of Kaiser. The other is a picture of a Liberty Ship.

At that time, it took an average of 226 days to build a ship. Through his genius and leadership, Kaiser reduced that time to an average of only 27 days. In an incredible display of genius, he actually constructed one ship, the Robert E. Perry, in just over four and a half days. Incredible! His shipyards built 1,383 merchant ships and 107 warships, and because of his entrepreneurial genius and ability to dream we won the war. At its peak, the Kaiser company employed 197,000 persons in ship-building.

Henry Kaiser did all of this because he lived out of the world inside of him. He believed that what others could not do because of the limitations of the world around them, he could do because he lived out of the greater world of vision, dreams, and destiny inside of him.

In speaking of the power that lies in the dreams and ideas of our heart and inner man, he spoke of how man can overcome the greatest obstacles around him:

"LIFE IS VERY SIMPLE. THERE ARE NOT ANY PROBLEMS, THERE ARE ONLY PROSPECTS! WHENEVER YOU HAVE BOTTLENECKS YOU HAVE OPPORTUNITIES!"

The amazing Henry Kaiser went on to express how much greater the world inside of him was than the world around him.

"IMPOSSIBLES ARE ONLY POSSIBLE AS THINKING MAKES THEM SO," he said and then added, "WHAT MAN CAN CONCEIVE AND IMAGINE, HE CAN ACCOMPLISH." Toward the end of his life, he realized one of his greatest dreams, which was to become one of the major manufacturers of cars in the world. To do so, he formed the Kaiser-Frazer Motor Car Corporation. It was what he called his biggest job. He was 63 years old when he began his dream of building cars. In 1946, he brought the first two cars he produced to the Waldorf Astoria Hotel in New York City. The huge overflow crowd that came to see his cars was so enthusiastic that they literally broke one of the hotel's huge glass doors. By September 1947, he had produced his 100,000th car. Six months later, he had produced 200,000 vehicles. It was an unprecedented and unheard of success in the field of manufacturing motor vehicles.

One of the forgotten parts of the Kaiser story is how the automobile business of Henry Kaiser was never a failure, but an amazing success. Although plagued by the lack of a V-8 engine, making his cars eventually fall behind in competition with the Big Three, Kaiser never gave up. Now that he had successfully built a company which produced over 700,000 automobiles and reached an amazing success level, Kaiser refused to be defeated. He knew that the power and dreams inside of him were greater than any circumstances around him. This was his plan, not only to survive, but to succeed in the automotive business for the rest of his life.

First because his automobile company was failing in the United States, in the 1960's he took the dies of the Kaiser automobile to Argentina and continued to make Kaisers for many years. Secondly, in a successful attempt to remain competitive in this tough business, he developed an idea to purchase the Willys Overland Company, maker of the Jeep. The company became the Kaiser Jeep company. It was, and is to this day, one of the most successful manufacturers of vehicles in the world. The Kaiser company actually made Jeeps until his death in 1967. Kaiser Jeep was sold by the Kaiser family to American Motors, and eventually to Chrysler. So to this day, people still celebrate the unconquerable spirit of Henry Kaiser every time they start their Jeep. If you think about it, Kaisers are being built all over the world until this day.

Kaiser lived by this unique statement of success always overcoming what seemed to be failure and the world inside of him always conquering the world around him. He said, "BEFORE YOU WORK YOURSELF OUT OF THE LAST JOB, LINE YOURSELF UP FOR A BIGGER ONE."

It was said that "Kaiser was always looking to line up a bigger job." No wonder--he always lived in the world inside of him, and it was always greater than the world around him.

*Chapter 13*

# THE DREAMERS
# WHO PUT
# THE WORLD ON WHEELS

The three decades of the 1840's, 1850's, 1860's produced perhaps the greatest generation of dreamers that ever graced this planet. These amazing dreamers created a new world that was to live in a dimension never imagined a few years previous to their births.

Their dream was a world where people would no longer be confined to the small world of previous generations but would be released to see and to interact with the whole world. They would be connected to that world not only through an expansion of their communication with others, but would also be free to move about from city to city, state to state, nation to nation through a system of motor driven vehicles that would operate on a network of highways that would connect city to city, state to state and nation to nation. These amazing men would create the automobile and the airplane. Nothing would ever be the same again.

This chapter would not be complete unless we honored them by sharing a very limited insight into these amazing men.

**CHARLES DURYEA:**
Born in 1861 in Canton, OH, he engineered the very first working American gasoline-powered automobile. He and his

brother, Frank built the first successful commercial automobile and were the first to incorporate an American business for the expressed purpose of building automobiles to sell to the general public. In 1893, they constructed and tested the first American automobile on the streets of Springfield, MA. In 1896 they founded the Dureyea Motor Wagon Company, the first to manufacture gasoline-powered vehicles. In 1896 they sold 13 cars and created a limousine that would be in production until the 1920's.

### RANSOM OLDS:

Born in 1864 in Geneva, OH, he created the first steam car and in 1896 his first gasoline-powered automobile. In 1899, he formed the Olds Motor Works and in 1901 created one of the first assembly lines.

### WILLIAM C. DURANT:

Born in 1861 in Boston, MA, he created a carriage-manufacturing company in 1886. He is best known as the founder of General Motors in 1908. Within two years, he lost control of the company he had created. He then formed the Chevrolet company with a friend, Louis Chevrolet, and their new company gained back control of General Motors.

### HARRY LELAND:

Born in 1843 in Barton, VT, he founded two major luxury brands, Cadillac and Lincoln. He sold Cadillac to General Motors and Lincoln to the Ford Motor Company.

### HENRY FORD:

Born in 1863 in Wayne County, MI, he incorporated the

Ford Motor Company in 1903. In 1908, he introduced the Model T that sold millions and initiated a new era in personal transportation. One of the major accomplishments of Henry Ford was to create an assembly line that would revolutionize the way that automobiles are manufactured.

### DAVID DUNBAR BUICK:

David Buick was born in 1854. In 1902 built his first car and in the same year organized the Buick Manufacturing Company. He is specifically credited with developing the overhead valve.

Talk about men who had a conflict between the world inside of them and the world around them! Think about the men who created the automobile.

Men such as Ransom Olds who built his first steam car in 1894 and his first gasoline automobile in 1896. Or William Durant who founded General Motors and Chrysler. Then there was Louis Chevrolet, automobile racer and founder of Chevrolet. The list would not be complete without Alfred Sloan or David Buick or Harry Leland, and Henry Ford. Most of these men were born in the 1850's or 1860's when there were no roads, no gas stations, or no parking lots. It was a world hostile to the automobile, and yet they dreamed.

Think about it for a moment. They had a dream. Their dream was to put America on wheels. When they first had that dream, the entire world around them was totally hostile to it.

But they lived in the world of destiny and dreams. They really believed the vision and dreams within them.

One day, one of them was riding with his father on top of a horse-drawn wagon when he had an encounter with destiny. He saw a portable engine and steam boiler that was mounted on wheels. It was moving slowly down the road and thrashing grain at the same time. A chain connected the wheels to the engine and to the rear wheels. The young man was off the wagon before his father could stop him and he began to shout questions to the fellow who was shoveling coal into the huge machine. That was a defining moment for this young man who had never seen an automobile. A world inside of him was being born.

On April 11, 1888, a family was busy with Holiday preparations. The young inventor lugged his first completed engine into the kitchen and mounted it on the sink. The flywheel was a hand wheel taken from a lathe. The crude carburetor was a metal container that simply let the gas drip. A piece of fiber with a wire through it served as a spark plug. That first engine was made out of bits and pieces of items that were in his shop. That day, an idea and a world was born in his head. His wife was asked to help start up the crude contraption. He connected the crude spark plug to the house's electric current. Clara was given the signal to start pouring gas into the crude carburetor. He turned a screw to let the gas trickle into the valve intake. The engine barked, and shook violently, but it worked! Now all that was left to build was a better engine and an automobile around it. That day, a new world of the automobile was fully created inside of him--he was off and running.

It was said that these young men had one foot in the 19th century, and one in the 20th. Their cars would replace the horse. One of them jokingly said, "Now we are going to get rid of the cow." They were always dreaming about something.

Most of them loved to be with other dreamers. For instance, Henry Ford had very close friendships with Thomas Edison, John Burroughs, department store titan John Wanamaker, and tire magnate Harvey Firestone. They made frequent camping trips together. In fact these dreamers actually had a name for their friendship calling themselves: "The Vagabonds."

Or we could take a look at the world of flight. The Wright brothers' father was a pastor and preacher. He taught from the pulpit that man would never fly, and yet his two sons had a dream that would change the world. Later, the Ford Motor Company built the first of 196 Ford Tri-Motor airplanes. The Ford Tin Goose and the Tri-Motor were the first all metal, multi-engine airplanes in the world. For many years, they were the standard equipment of all commercial airlines until the flight of the Boeing 247 in 1933. For this writer, it is interesting that the first commercial flights in the world took place with the old Ford Tri-motor between the cities of Detroit, Buffalo, and Cleveland.

In 1910, the automobile industry was already making the famed Model T. The public clamored to own one. The industry decided on a revolutionary concept. Instead of bringing the man to work, work would be brought to the man.

1913 saw a breakthrough initiated. A new way of bringing component parts together was attempted in the flywheel department. The operation was divided into 29 separate steps. Workers were instructed to place only one part in the assembly before pushing the flywheel down the line to the next employee. Previously, it had taken one employee about 20 minutes to assemble a flywheel magneto. Now, 29 men finished the job in 13 minutes.

Further advances trimmed it to five minutes. Gradually this process was applied to the construction of the engine and other parts, and of course, eventually to the entire automobile.

These pioneers of the automobile had brought a revolution

to the manufacturing process.

Those dreamers who faced a world around them without roads, gas stations or parking lots, had another entirely new and different world inside of them.

Engage in the conflicts between the two worlds and create another world around you.

These were men who dreamed a dream and discovered that true greatness and true success come from the power of a dream inside of us. They truly believed in the dream and as a result changed the entire world.

## THE DREAM WORKBOOK
## QUESTIONS ON CHAPTERS 12 and 13

1.    The men who developed the automobile saw a WORLD INSIDE OF THEM that was on motorized WHEELS but the world around them was HOSTILE to their dream. Describe the difference between the dream inside of them and the world around them.

_____

_____

_____

_____

_____

_____

_____

_____

_____

2.   Name some of the men who put the world on wheels.

1.   _____

2.   _____

3.   _____

4.   _____

6,.   _____

3.   All of these men shared one thing in common, they all had a DREAM.  Write a few words to describe their dream.

_____

_____

_____

_____

_____

_____

_____

_____

_____

_____

_____

_____

_____

_____

*Chapter 14*

# PROFILE OF
# A WORLD CHANGER
# -
# GOD SENDS A MAN
# TO CREATE A NEW WORLD

## *THE STORY OF SAMUEL*

When God wants to do a "new thing" on the earth, He finds a man or woman who has "world changer" possibilities in his heart. This person was already in the pre-destined plan of God before the foundation of the earth. So it was in the time when the people of God needed a leader who would change their circumstances and bring them to their eternal destiny as the nation of Israel, when God's people were seeking to have a king like other nations. That person was already in the mind of God, but was not physically alive at that time.

God, therefore, put it in the heart of a young and barren woman by the name of Hannah to give birth to a son. Hannah was not just praying for a son to love and enjoy the wonder of her motherly love, but desired to give birth to the plan and purpose of God on the earth. Year-by-year, her desire grew stronger until the dream of God inside of her obsessed her entire being. Each year, she went to Jerusalem to pray in the Temple, and pour out these desires to God for a son.

One year, the High Priest, Eli saw her praying. She was so intent in her prayers that Eli thought she was drunk. She answered that she had not consumed anything that would make her drunken, but that she was pouring forth from her inner being a desire to have a son. However, it was not just a barren woman desiring a child, but Hannah was pouring forth the desire of God to birth His servant who would fulfill His will here on earth.

Although Hannah did not understand the passion inside her heart, she realized that she was really desperate for the birth of a son. As Eli left her, he turned back long enough to acknowledge that the God of heaven would answer her prayers. Within a year, her son was born--an answer to the intercession of this woman of God.

They called the child Samuel. He was born as a child of destiny and purpose. He would prepare the world for the birth of a Messiah who would be the monarch and king of the entire universal creation. Let's take the journey with him.

The journey begins with a miracle. Hannah did not have the physical ability to bear a child. But, every impossibility was defeated, and she gave birth to a perfect child! A journey of destiny always begins with a miracle. Mine began with a miracle of birth when my mother could not have a child under normal circumstances. I was in reality a miracle child my mother otherwise would not have.

God invades His world with miracles. Many people who have changed their world began their journey with the miracle of existence.

## GOD USES WHAT BELONGS TO HIM

When I read the story of Samuel, it is an amazing picture of my family and my life. After the miracle of birth, Hannah immediately begins the process of giving her child back to God. She not only dedicates him to God with prayer, but she actually brings him back to the Temple and presents him to the priest as a servant of the priest and of God.

It has been my observation that not all, but many of the great men and women who have been used by God in a supernatural way, have been blessed by parents who knew how to present their child back to God. This was truly the experience of young Hannah and her little son, Samuel.

## SAMUEL CAME TO THE EARTH AT A TIME OF CRISIS

God has a timing for everything. There was a special reason why God so moved the heart of Hannah to have a passion for birthing a son. It was specifically related to the fact that the world was in a time of spiritual crisis.

When I think of Samuel coming into the world in a day of spiritual, moral, and political crisis, I am reminded of the story of Winston Churchill during World War II.

A few years before the outbreak of the war, a young woman was a nanny for a child by the name of Winston. She was a Christian and was of the strong conviction that the child for which she was responsible had come to the earth with a great purpose. She constantly told young Winston that he was special and that he is on earth for a specific reason. Again and again, she passionately shared the truth of his Divine appointment with the young Winston.

The young man grew and entered the political arena. During his rise to power, England and the world approached the beginning of World War II. Young Winston, remembering the words and prayers of his nanny, came to believe he was a man on a divine assignment.

This man of destiny, Winston Churchill, was absolutely responsible for the victories of the Allied forces during World War II.

Samuel was the Winston Churchill of his day. The world was in crisis. A mother prayed for a child. She gave that child to God when he was very small and brought him to the Temple, presenting him to the High Priest for service,.

It was here that Samuel heard the voice of God. It was here that he began his ministry. And in the end, it was Samuel who anointed the first king of the people of God. It was Samuel who was sent by God to the house of Jesse where he found David, a shepherd boy, and anointed him as king.

Most of all, it was Samuel who established the throne of David as an eternal throne. It was Samuel who anointed that insignificant shepherd to sit on an eternal throne!

## THE MIRACLE OF THE CALL

The voice of God is described in Scripture as God coming to the Temple. The Scripture says, "Then God came and stood before him." (I Samuel 3:10)

After hearing a voice calling his name a few times, Samuel went to Eli, the High Priest. Eli tells the boy to say to the voice, "Speak, Lord, for thy servant hears." When the boy recognizes God's voice, the God of heaven and earth reveals His plan to Samuel.

The remarkable part of this story is that, unlike the average human being, Samuel heard God's voice. When God is about to bring change to the face of the earth, He looks for a man or woman who hears God's voice.

It is this part of the story of Samuel that illustrates my point to you. God has placed His dream and His voice inside of you. The Bible talks about the still, small voice. We must listen to the voice. It is in the voice that there is Divine wisdom and Divine direction. That voice is the Holy Spirit of God, and the mind of Christ.

## *Chapter 15*

# MAKING FRIENDS WITH THE WORLD AROUND YOU

Thusfar, we have discussed the conflict between the world within you and the world around you. We have seen the two worlds as enemies of each other. In one dimension, this is possible. However, the world around you is not your enemy. The world around you is the world you are destined to influence and change. What is our relationship with that world that we have to live in, breathe in, work in, worship in, and just live. The world around us is a magnificent world. It gives us a place to live, a place to play, and a place to fulfill our destiny before God. It is the very world for which God has given us a destiny to change and influence as light and salt.

When God comes to us, as He did to Samuel, and challenges us with a predestined work to do, how do we respond, and how do we relate to the world around us?

One day a woman came into my office and told me of her vision to start a children's home. She had no money, no sponsors, just a vision that she believed was from God.

I said to her: "There are a lot of things you have to do before you start a children's home. You have money problems, legal challenges, and you lack an understanding of the laws that govern children's homes. Why don't you begin by going down to the Department of Social Services to serve children who need foster care? You could reach out to five or six foster children and begin your ministry immediately."

*The World Inside Of You*
*Is the Seed That You Must Plant*
*In The World Around You*

# THE WORLD INSIDE OF YOU IS THE SEED YOU MUST PLANT IN THE WORLD AROUND YOU

We now come to the "how to" section of this book. We have talked about the tension there is between the world inside of you and the existing world around you. Now we want to share where these two worlds meet.

These two worlds are not enemies of each another. In fact, the very world that God has placed inside of you is designed by God for the world around you, where you are to bring the wonder and the creativity of the Kingdom of God.

This section of "The Conflict" is to assist you in the discovery of how the world of dreams and visions inside of you is given to you by God to change the world around you. Therefore, the two worlds are not in conflict with each other. It is you and I, who attempt to bring the world inside of us to the world around us, who create conflict. The tension between the ever present now and the overwhelming world of the Spirit of God is the center of the conflict.

So, let us approach this discussion with hope and faith that the world inside of us is given to us by God to invade the world around us and bring the wonder of the Kingdom of God that Jesus said was "within us."

## Chapter 16

# GOD BUILT A CATHEDRAL FOR YOUR DREAM

L ittle thirteen-year-old Eva literally skipped into her parents' bedroom, almost in tears. Her father glanced up, observing her demeanor and the tears that now ran down her face. Her Dad, Ivan Q. Spencer, one of the great leaders of the early Pentecostal movement, was aware that something was happening in his little girl's heart. In her own words, she said, "A longing churned within me that I needed to express." She said, "Daddy, I want to be a missionary." Her wise father replied, "In the Lord's time we will see about it."

What amazing words of wisdom. It would be many years before it was the Lord's time. She would marry, give birth to three children, (one who would die at birth) and spend several years serving the Lord in America. It would be 21 years later that she would set sail for a five-week voyage to Africa on the USS America. But it all began on that special day when a thirteen-year-old girl heard the voice of the Lord that she would be a missionary. In Africa, she would do an amazing work among the Massai tribes in the nation of Kenya.

Perhaps, like little Eva, there is a dream inside of you. In your heart, you really believe the dream. But just how does this work? How do I live my life so the dream inside of me will find fulfillment? How do I live in the world around me and yet believe in the dream inside me? How do I live in the world inside me and at the same time live life in the world around me which seems to contradict the world inside of me?

What if I were to tell you that the world around us is in reality our friend, the very world that God intends for us to change with the dream inside of us?

After all, the world of dreams inside you is not an enemy of the world around you. The world inside you is a seed that needs to be planted. The world around you is the field where the seed needs to be planted. The seed is useless without the field, and the field has no value without the seed.

When I ask myself how I am to relate to the world around me, I first of all tell myself that what is inside of me is intended for the world around me. I tell myself that when I plant my dream in the soil of the world around me, the world around me will become like the world inside of me.

Remember the story of Abram. God comes to this son of an idol-maker and describes a very different world than the one where Abram lives. He talks to him about a new land where he is to go and raise the family that only exists in his dreams. Where does Abram go with his dreams?

Abram goes where all of us have to go with our dreams. Dreams can never become physical realities until we take them to the physical world around us. First of all, God takes Abram for a walk on the beach. I have found that is one of the best places to go with my dreams. My step-mother used to have a lovely home in Clearwater Beach, FL. It was just a five minute walk from her front door to beautiful Clearwater Beach. Like Abram, I used to walk on that beach with my dreams. Dreams incubate well on a beach.

Abram took his dream and walked on the beach. The more he walked, the more vivid became his dream. This man who was without child and had almost no hope of fathering a child, began to walk through the sand, dreaming with every step he took. On a real beach, in a real physical world, suddenly God encounters this man of faith. God encourages him to take a prayer position. He gets on his knees, almost like a mother about to give birth to a child. In this child-bearing position, God takes him by the hand and speaks into his spirit. The Bible tells us that God tells him to scoop up a handful of sand, and as he holds the sand in his hand, hundreds of little crystals of sand begin to filter back to the ground. God says to the dreamer, "Number the sand, if you can, this is the number of children I will give you; they shall number as the sand of the sea."

As the sun sets, and Abram continues to think on the things that God is saying, he looks up into the sky. The night stars become like thousands of little beacons of light, and again the voice God comes to Abram, "and your children shall be like the stars of the heaven, and like the stars too many to even number."

I believe that one of the first places we are to go with our dreams is where we are part of the creation of God. It is in the beauty of nature that we can discover in our prayer time and communication with God, the most open door to the visions and dreams of God.

I remember an evening in Maui when Wanda and I were spending four days with my friend, Dr. Robert Schuller. Not only is Robert Schuller a great man of God, but all of us know him as a great dreamer. As the sun began to set, we were walking in the backyard of the famed Baldwin estate and came to a clearing where there was a simple and rustic platform made of old wood. At the front of the platform was a small rustic and crude pulpit. Dr. Schuller made his way to the rough-hewn pulpit, and in typical Robert Schuller fashion, raised his hands to heaven, looked up at the cloudless sky where the stars were soon to appear, and the builder of the Crystal Cathedral said words I will never forget: "This open space under God's heaven with no roof or barrier between us and God is the GREATEST CATHEDRAL IN THE WORLD!" Since that day, for this writer, there is not a venue that is closer to God in the world than the open heaven.

So here, in a place of openness and without a roof between Abram and his God, he hears God speak into his heart. For the first time, he is aware of the greatness of the miracle that God is about to bring to his life and produce through his body.

I want to suggest to you that when God gives you a dream for His world, take that dream to the place of its final fulfillment. You see, your dream is meant for the world, and it is difficult to really examine or define it when you are hidden away in some seemingly spiritual building. Church buildings are great for worship, but dreams are easier to examine when you are out under the canopy of heaven.

It was my good friend, Lester Sumrall, one of the greatest dreamers in the history of the world, who took me to a park bench on the famed Luneta Park on Manila Bay. As we sat on the bench under the open heaven, this great man of God said to his young protege, "When I had a very small church, but there was a church of thousands in my heart, I used to come to this bench, sit here for hours and dream the dream that was inside of me. I would say to God, 'God give me a place in this city.'"

The story of Lester Sumrall building a church of thousands as a result of an unbelievable miracle is now history. But that dream was incubated under an open heaven on the bench overlooking Manila Bay. It was here that faith in his heart was born.

So take your dream to your own Manila Bay. Get someplace where you can feel the breeze, bask in the sun, and touch the beauty of nature. Go to the world that God has called you to, and there the dream will incubate into reality.

I want to suggest that not only did Abraham go to the open heavens to dream and pray, but many other great men in the scripture went to their "Bethel" or mountain where they could see and hear things from God's perspective, including Jesus Himself who often went to the mountain to commune with the Father.

Not only does this concept have Biblical roots, but according to some of the world's great thinkers, they also suggest scientific proof for this theory. Richard Neutra, one of the greatest architects of all time, suggests this in what he calls the "Architechtural philosophy called Bio-Realism."

Neutra states that "Man is a spiritual creature designed to receive messages from God and communicate his thoughts to God." He goes on to state that this communication was to take place in the "habitat" that God created for him. Here in the garden, man would be creative and here he would hear God's voice.

Another man by the name of Rene' Dubos discovered that biological organisms have sociological behavior. Dubos said that "every biological organism lives in its own sociological environment." He went on to say that if you change the environment, then you will kill the organism. However, before the organism dies, it will become deviant, adjusting downward in its struggle to survive. He believed, along with Neutra, that this is also true with the human being. If you change his environment, he will continue to live for a period of time; however, he will also become deviant and in his effort to survive will spiral down to adjust to his new environment.

Both of these scientific minds believed that man was created to live under an open heaven in the garden. A garden under an open heaven was his natural habitat. If man is moved out of the garden, he, like all other forms of organisms, will, in an effort to survive, adjust downward. Take the human being out of this open heaven environment, put him among concrete, asphalt, power poles, sirens, squealing brakes and gunfire, and he will adjust downward. In this new but inferior environment, we cannot hear God clearly and the window to the voice of heaven is no longer audible.

Both of these scientific minds believe that God speaks best and most clearly under an open heaven. Most always I go to where the stars, the clouds, the sun, the beauty of the heavenly realm can be seen, and where the voice of God is more clearly heard. I would suggest, that IS our "Cathedral."

It was Neutra who was the architect for the Crystal Cathedral. My close and wonderful friend, Dr. Robert Schuller believed the same. Therefore, he called on Richard Neutra to design a church where thousands would worship under the open heaven.

That is why for almost sixty years I have always enjoyed driving a convertible. Nothing compares with putting the top down, letting the breeze blow through your hair, and feeling the sunshine on you, with nothing between God's voice and you. Suddenly, I experience the wonder of communion when my friend Jesus slips into the seat of that open convertible with me. Nothing keeps Him from me, for I have been in His Cathedral, under the open heaven.

No wonder Lester Sumrall went to that little beach on Manila Bay and dreamed, and no wonder his dreams came true.

# THE DREAM WORK BOOK
## QUESTIONS ON CHAPTER 16

1. Abraham took the DREAM that God put in his heart to the OPEN CATHEDRAL OF AN OPEN HEAVEN. While he walked on the BEACH, stopped and knelt down and put the sand around him in his hand, he began to COUNT THE SANDS. When he did, his DREAM CAME ALIVE. Take a moment and describe where you can go to dream God's dream under the canopy of an open heaven.

_____

_____

_____

_____

_____

_____

_____

_____

2. Abraham's next step was to look at the expanse of God's open Cathedral, and he began to COUNT THE STARS. The dream in his heart took on new life. Describe how you believe Abraham felt inside of him.

_____

_____

_____

_____

_____

_____

_____

_____

_____

_____

_____

3.    The first place we take the dream is to the open air of GOD'S CATHEDRAL, and there we DREAM AND SEE OUR DREAM COME ALIVE INSIDE OF US. Make a written statement as to where you will take your dream.

_____

_____

_____

_____

_____

_____

_____

_____

_____

*Chapter 17*

# BUILDING AN ALTAR FOR YOUR DREAM

After God has given the dream to Abram in Genesis 12:1, he proposes a covenant between Abram and God. Abram has several responses. One of Abram's first responses is found in Genesis 12:7, HE BUILDS AN ALTAR!

When God began to give me a dream for my life, even as a child, I intuitively knew that I needed to connect this dream to God in a very specific way. In the natural I could not speak, for I was a hopeless stutterer. I did not have the personality of a preacher, being shy and almost afraid of my own shadow. And I was very sickly. What was I to do with the dream to be a preacher and touch the world? My dream would require supernatural provision.

Since the dream was so far from natural possibilities, and I did not have the natural ability or talents to become the man in my dream, I knew that my only hope was the supernatural. So, I began taking my dream to an altar, and building altars where I could touch the very face of God. I intuitively knew that this dream was far beyond my own ability, and the only way I could even touch my dream was to touch God.

My first altar was beside my mother's bed. It was there that my Godly mother taught me the wonder of the Cross and the sacrificial death of my Savior. It was there at that altar where I learned how to pray. It was truly my first altar.

My second altar was in that small, insignificant, and almost unknown Assemblies of God church on Elm Street in East Aurora, NY. That little church with its handmade seats and its two old 8' X 10' worn carpets with two crude handmade benches became my altar. I could not wait until I got to church on Sunday night to kneel and worship my Lord at this altar. To this day, I cannot wait until it is time to go to church on Sunday night, for that is where I still find this same altar.

You see, I still need Him to bring the dreams God still gives me to pass as much as I needed Him when I was a child with unbelievable dreams inside of me. In those days, I could not wait until the preacher finished his sermon. When he finished and invited us to pray, I would go to my altar and communicate with the God who was going to take this incapable child and make him into a preacher. I knew that was not possible in the natural, so the only place it could happen was at the altar of God.

Dreams are made by God to be surrendered and molded at an altar where God is present. It is to these altars that we must take our dream, and there it will be developed. It is there that we will birth new dreams that will fulfill the major dream of God for our lives.

Abraham was so right. If the dream that God had placed in his heart was really true and would one day find fulfillment, the only way was for the man with the dream inside of him to take it to the altar where he would communicate with God. It was here at the altar of prayer that the giver of the dream would make the recipient of the dream ready to become the fulfillment of the dream.

There is a source of empowerment in your life for the dream that God has given you. That source is not human talent, education, or human partnership. The source of empowerment for your dream is to build a partnership with your God.

Make prayer the central focus of your life. Prayer is not boring, prayer is, in reality, dreaming God's dreams and thinking God's thoughts. What an exciting time prayer can be when it is a time to really enter into the very mind of our Lord.

You have the mind of Christ.,In His mind is everything you need to create the wonder of the world He has commissioned you to create. Partner with Him. Dream His dreams. Become a partner with Him in the intimacy of prayer. Then, take His dream and His creativity and create the dream inside of you in the world around you.

## THE DREAM WORKBOOK
## QUESTIONS ON CHAPTER 17

1. The second thing that Abraham did was to BUILD AN ALTAR. God's dreams begin to grow within us when we worship Him and enter into His PRESENCE. Describe where you will go to build your altar.

_____

_____

_____

_____

_____

_____

_____

2.    Pastor Reid went to the little Pentecostal church every Sunday night and knelt there sometimes for hours. Here he built his altar and it was here that God gave him his dreams for the future. Take a moment to WRITE YOUR COMMITMENT to do what Abraham did and BUILD YOUR ALTAR OF PRAYER. Make a written commitment to do it and to go there every day.

_____

_____

_____

_____

_____

_____

_____

_____

Lord Jesus, this day I commit myself to build an altar and spend enough time in your presence so that you will give me Your dreams.


_____

YOUR SIGNATURE

## Chapter18

# RECOGNIZE THE SOURCE OF YOUR DREAM

Thousands of years ago God created a man and named him Adam. This man was created in the very image of God. He was his father's child. He thought like God, he did things like God did, he had within him the wonder of the creative power of his heavenly creative Father.

God gave this man two specific tasks. The first was to tend the garden and the second was to subdue the earth. Subduing the earth would mean that Adam and God would have to create a partnership, and together they would extend the wonder and the order of the garden to the rest of the earth.

We know the story. Instead of following the job description that God had prepared for him, Adam decided to disobey God. In this book, we will not discuss the mistake, but let's take a look at what might have been. What if Adam had followed the instructions of God and the creativity that God had placed inside of him, coupled with the woman that God would give as his partner? Even we cannot imagine what our world would have looked like today.

However, the mandate is still the same today. We have been commissioned by God to recreate God's world. When the disciples asked Jesus how to pray, Jesus gave them a model prayer. The first request that Jesus told us to ask of our heavenly Father was, "THY KINGDOM COME, THY WILL BE DONE, ON EARTH AS IT IS IN HEAVEN." Do you realize that the mandate of the first part of the book of Genesis is the same for the redeemed man as it was for the first man?

However, we cannot do that by ourselves. We may be made in the image of God, but we also know that it is far beyond us to fulfill the mandate He has given us without our becoming His partner.

I want to suggest to you that we are "Partners with God," and the only way we can possibly fulfill His instructions to take what is inside of us and recreate the world around us is by becoming His partner.

In the Garden of Eden, God gave specific instructions to Adam: He had permission to use anything in that Garden except for one tree. He could enjoy the beauty of that tree, he could sit under its shade, but he was not to eat of it. It was off limits.

God made it "off limits" as the absolute symbol of the ownership of God. It was the symbol that God owned the garden, and Adam was simply a steward. To not touch the tree was like a man being paid by an employer a certain amount of money. He then would take a specific portion of that salary to pay rent to the owner of the property where he lived. If you live in a rental property, you take a specific amount or percentage of your salary and give it to the landlord for the right to live in it for another month. Only when you pay the rent do you have the right to live in that house or apartment another month.

Every time that Adam did not touch the forbidden tree, he was saying to God, "that tree is the symbol that God owns this garden. God is letting me use it to live in, but when I do not touch the fruit of that tree, I say to God that He is the owner of this garden, and I am simply the steward of His garden." Not touching the produce of the forbidden tree, Adam was telling

God, "This is my rent on your garden, and now I have a right to the garden for another period of time."

So it was also with what the Scripture calls the tithe. It is called in the Hebrew Scriptures "the sacred portion" or "the forbidden portion" or the "cursed portion." Bringing the tithe to God is saying to God, "I live on this earth; I am a steward. You are the owner, and my only rights are the recognition of Your ownership."

If you are going to be a world changer, if you are going to take the dreams and the abilities that God has placed inside of you to change the world around you, then you first of all must recognize the ownership of God.

What does He own? He owns the dream! He owns the world for which the dream was made! He owns the creativity that will produce the dream! You and I are simply stewards of the dream, stewards of His creativity, and stewards of the world for which the dream was made.

I must do something to show God who is the owner and who is the steward. Abraham recognized the ownership of God in this way. He was under the spiritual authority of a Priest called Melchizedek. Genesis 14:18-20 tells us that Abraham brought a tenth of everything he had to this priest. When Abraham did this, he sent a message to God and to all the creation of the universe. That message said simply this: God owns this world, God owns the dreams He has placed inside of me, and owns the creativity that is in me to plant the world inside of me in the world around me. When I bring my tithes to the priest, I am declaring God's full ownership of His world, my dreams, and all of the creativity that is inside of me.

Abraham's story makes us realize that a step to fulfilling our dreams is the bringing of the tithe to God.

# NOTES

_____

_____

_____

_____

_____

_____

_____

_____

_____

_____

_____

_____

_____

_____

_____

_____

_____

_____

## *Chapter 19*

# BUILDING A WORLD OF GENEROSITY FOR THE DREAM

God is so good. When I look at my life I am always amazed at how generous God has been with me. He defines His people as a "blessed people," and we are. I love to tell people how blessed I am. After living for God for over 75 years, I am a living testimony to the blessings of God.

I believe that if we are to find true and complete fulfillment of our dreams, we must become a generous people. To some of us this comes naturally. To others, it is not so easy. In fact, Abram probably found generosity somewhat difficult, especially in the story that is told in Genesis 13.

The problem in chapter 13 is blessing. Both Abraham and Lot, who were living under the covenant of God, were blessed beyond measure. The problem was that there was, literally, too much blessing. The beautiful land became insufficient for the herds of both Abram and Lot.

Blessing always creates problems. Sometimes we are driven by a desire for blessing. But blessing comes with its own issues. For Abram and Lot the blessing of God upon their flocks was so great that even the beautiful and fruitful land was insufficient for both of them. It was like two farmers whose barns were not big enough for the harvest.

They knew that if they both stayed on the land, their flocks would starve. They knew that both of them together could not survive.

The truth was that only generosity could solve the problem. So Abram made a proposal. Knowing what his answer would be, and that he would have to give the best land to Lot, he simply asked Lot what he wanted. He told Lot that whatever portion he wanted, he would take the remaining portion.

Of course, Lot wanted the well-watered portion where his flock would flourish. Abram immediately knew that he would have to take his flocks to a place where there would not be sufficient food. Under ordinary circumstances, his flocks would die.

Was this a test by God? I suppose it was. Was this a trick question created by God? Of course not. The answer to this problem would show where true riches are kept by God. They are not in the well-watered plains of abundance, for this abundance can dissipate in a few months' time without rain. Abundance is only in the realm of the Divine.

For Abram, the question was source. For Lot, the source of blessing was the land. For Abram, the source of blessing was God. Abram knew something Lot did not know. Because Abram knew the source of the blessing, he was not afraid to be generous so he gave to Lot this valuable piece of land. He knew the source of blessing was not the land, but the God who made the land.

## THE DREAM WORKBOOK
## QUESTIONS ON CHAPTERS 18 and 19

1. What does it mean to me when I pray, *"Thy Kingdom Come, thy will be done on earth as it is in heaven?"*

2. What is God asking me to *"recreate on the earth?"*

3. Why is the tithe the symbol of the ownership of God on the earth?

4. What did Abraham know about God that Lot did not know?

*Chapter 20*

# THE TRANSCENDENCE OF THE DREAM

How powerful is the dream inside of your heart? Is it powerful enough to overcome the huge obstacles that will attempt to defeat it during your lifetime? Or is there an inherent power in that dream that is capable of overcoming anything in this world, even the very power of persons and the hostile environment where the dream is intended by the sovereignty of God to flourish and grow?

One of the facts that we must put into this evaluation is when was the destiny and dream inside of you created? The Scripture gives us interesting insight into this very relevant question. Let me quote to you a few verses:

**Revelation 17:8** (AV)
"Whose names were not written in the book of life from the foundation of the world." (This verse indicates that there are this whose very names, identity, and destiny were chosen and created by God for a specific purpose before the very creation of the earth.)

**Hebrews 4:3** (AV)
"Although the works were finished from the foundation of the world."

**Ephesians 1:4** (AV)
"According as He has chosen us in Him before the foundation of the world.

**John 17:24** (AV)

"Those whom thou hast given me be with me where I am; that they may behold my glory, which thou hast given me: for **thou lovest me before the foundation of the world.**"

**I Peter 1:20** (AV)

"Who verily was foreordained before the foundation of the world."

The truth that is evident in these verses is simply that Jesus was chosen--and we were chosen in Him and foreordained in Him--before the foundation of the world. That means God actually chose us and wrote our names before He made the very first piece of matter. Before there was a constellation, before there was a planet or a star. Before there was a mountain or a sea, or a tree, or an animal, or a bird, God actually created your person and destiny and wrote your name or destiny in His book.

Remember the dream, destiny and purpose that God has placed in your heart. It was made before the foundation of the world and programmed or predestined into the very act of creation. It is superior to and has power over creation itself.

It is like the little seed of grass that is under a concrete sidewalk. Left alone long enough, the superiority and power of that seed will crack the strength of concrete and suddenly one day will push so against the concrete itself that it will actually crack, and the superior power of the blade of grass will break through and touch the beauty of the light of the sun!

Every time I come to the realization of a dream that God has placed inside of me, I say to myself, "That destiny and dream was created before the foundation of the universe." That little idea seed that I just discovered inside of me was put there by God when He wrote my name and destiny in His book. It is superior to and greater than any force in the created universe. Therefore, it has the power to overcome, the power to break through any barrier in the universe. I look forward to the day when the concrete world around my dream will crack, and the dream will truly manifest itself into the light of God's creation.

The Scripture itself has been given to us so that we may discover the power of our destiny and dream. Did you realize that before God created any matter He wrote the name of Joseph into His plan for His creation? God knew that the famine would come to a nation in Egypt and that nation would be part of His plan of redemption of the universe. He also knew before the foundation of the world that there would be a nation called Israel that needed to be saved. Therefore, in His divine plan of redemption He knew that there must be a Joseph who would present His plan to the monarch of Egypt to save His nation during the famine.

God wrote you and your destiny into His plan and tapestry for His universe before He made the world. If you believe that, you will realize how important your life and destiny is to God.

In the light of that truth, let me quote some of those Scriptures as I read them in the Bible for myself: "According as He hath chosen *Tommy Reid*, in Him before the foundation of the world (Eph 1:4) and has written the name of *Tommy Reid* in the book of life before the foundation of the world (Revelation 17:8), and has finished His work before the foundation of the world (Hebrews 4:3) and that the life, ministry, destiny and purpose of *Tommy Reid* was foreordained before the foundation of the world (I Peter 1:20)."

When the purpose and destiny of God begins to grow as a

seed inside of me and seems powerless and weak, I will speak to that seed to keep growing, keep developing. I let that seed know that buried deep inside its very essence is the preordained purposes of God for His universe. I tell it to keep growing, continually envisioning it breaking through the concrete world of God's universe, until it begins to take root and change the world around it. And, I will continually give it light and water, and  fertilize it with my faith so it will grow into an idea that will change the world.

## Chapter 21

# Dreams Make The Impossible Become The Inevitable

George Danzig was one of the greatest mathematicians in the world. But he did not begin there. His greatness was discovered by accident.

George went to college during the Great Depression. One day, he heard a rumor. It was not his love or brilliance in mathematics that caused him to make the decision, it was his need for money.

He heard that the person who got the highest grade in class would be given a job as an assistant teacher, and he needed the job because he needed money. He was desperate.

George went home and studied very hard. In fact so hard and so long that on the day of the scheduled test, he was late for class. Coming into class at the last minute, he stopped by the professor's desk and picked up his test paper. On that paper were eight problems. During the class period, he solved all eight.

As he started to leave, he saw two more problems on the blackboard. He decided to stay a few more minutes to solve the problems, assuming they were part of the test. Unable to find the answers, he took them home. Day after day, he worked on those two problems. Tuesday, Wednesday, Thursday, and most of Friday he worked. Finally, he solved both and took them back to his teacher. He could not find the professor, so he left the answers on his desk.

On Sunday morning, the professor came to his house, knocked on the door, and when George opened the door, the he excitedly said, "George, you made mathematics history!" He asked George if he had to come to class late that day and if he had heard his explanation of the two questions. George told the professor that he had come late and did not hear him explain them.

The professor said, "George, I didn't put those questions on the blackboard as part of the test. I put them there because they were two problems that no one has ever solved. Even Einstein attempted them and could not find the answers. George, you solved them both!"

George looked as his professor and said, "If I had not been late for class and heard you say that these two problems had never been solved and that even Einstein had tried but did not succeed, I would have believed I could not solve them either, and would never have attempted to solve them."

George Danzig became one of the greatest mathematicians in the world because he was not confined by his fears or his unbelief.

To whom are you choosing to listen, the people who say it cannot be done because no one has ever done it, or the words of our Lord who said, "All things are possible if you believe."

When I came to Buffalo everyone believed that there would never be a Pentecostal revival in the Catholic Church. No one ever believed that over 100,000 Roman Catholic people in the Buffalo diocese would be filled with the Holy Spirit like the people at Azusa Street in 1906. When I believed that the impossible was becoming a reality, we experienced a revival that shook this city.

Even when it was happening, many in the Pentecostal church still did not believe. They still saw it as impossible. When I believed that what I was seeing in the Catholic Church was the same revival I saw in my dreams at that little Pentecostal altar fifty years earlier in my life, my church exploded in growth from less than 150 people to more than 700 in one week! What I had seen in the Spirit became a reality.

The truth of the matter is that the dream in your heart may seem impossible, but in God what is impossible becomes the inevitable. God saw it. God showed you what He saw. And now, you stand between the belief that the dream is impossible and the truth that the dream is inevitable. It was written by God before the foundation of the world. God destined for it to happen.....JUST BELIEVE IT!

## Chapter 22

# DREAM WITH ME

This is the final chapter of my portion of this book. It is the chapter that is important for you to complete. This chapter will be the answers to several questions:

1. What is the dream inside of you?
2. When was it written?
3. When and how did you discover it?
4. When did you believe it?
5. What steps am I taking to make the dream come true?
6. Where will I go daily to dream God's dream?
7. Where will I build my altar to let God grow the dream in my heart?
8. I will record the daily, weekly, monthly, and yearly progress of my dream.

Begin writing! This book would not be complete without you writing this chapter. I cannot write it for you. I cannot make this discovery for you. This is between you and God.

You must hear His voice and write down what He has said to you. Do not fail going to a place under the open heaven where you can dream the expansiveness of the dream inside of you. Let the sands of the earth run through your fingers and count the magnitude of the dream. Look up at the heavens, count the stars, and let the dream expand inside of you.

Earlier in this book, I referred to the day God healed me when I was crippled with polio. I remember the morning I woke and heard the voice of God. Those words were never to be forgotten, "TODAY IS THE DAY I WILL HEAL YOU!" I heard the words and believed them. I called my mother to my bedside and asked her to call our Pastor telling her if he would come and pray for me I would be healed today. She called, and he could not come. She walked back in the room and told me the disappointing news. I was totally devastated. But as she walked out of the room, I heard the voice of Jesus again speak to me these words, "TOMMY, THE PASTOR IS NOT HERE, BUT I AM JESUS. I AM HERE, AND I WILL HEAL YOU".

Hearing His voice brought not only hope but faith and healing to me. I pulled myself up to the side of the bed, pulled my body to a standing position, and reached out and took His hand. As I took hold of that hand, I began to walk. With every step I held on tighter. And as I walked across the floor and ran the stairs for the first time since I had contracted polio, I said to myself, "I will never let go of that hand."

That day, I learned my greatest lesson in reaching my destiny. First, I heard His voice. I responded to that voice by telling Jesus who spoke to me that I was listening and would do what He said to me. But I also determined I would keep listening for His voice the rest of my life. It would guide me for as long as I lived.

Then as I took my first step and felt the caress of His nail-scarred hand as He led me across the floor to walk, I told Him that I would never let go of His hand. It would lead me the rest of my life. And it has.

As you walk toward your destiny, listen for His voice and obey what He says. Secondly, take His hand and never let it go.

Nothing will ever be greater and more life-changing than His voice and His hand.

What a journey! Nothing can be more exciting. Yes, write this chapter yourself.

**HAPPY JOURNEY!**

*How to Live
Out of a Dream*

**~ perspective from the next generation ~**

---

*A Legacy of
Dreams*

**By Rev. Aimee L. Reid-Sych**

# Commanding Your Post

## Rev. Aimee L. Reid-Sych

Dreams are eternal by nature. They outlive the dreamer. The beauty of it is that portions of our dreams are destined to be fulfilled in subsequent generations. This is how we leave a legacy. We transfer the core heart of our dream to the next generation.

One of my greatest privileges in life is to walk alongside my father, Bishop Reid, in seeing his many dreams come to pass.

The endless deposits he has made in my life can be summed up in one sentence:   He has taught me to dream!

I invite you to hear my heart as the next generation dreamer as I reveal my perspective in these final chapters.  It is time. You and I must arise and ...

"Command Our Post!"

### Chapter 23

# POST VS PURPOSE
# Introduction:
# "Commanding Your Post"

What is your post? What is that place that God has ordained for you to command?

This is not a passive place; it is a place of power, of authority, of fulfillment. It is a place where God is truly working and moving within you. It is not contingent upon circumstance, nor is it contingent upon your feelings or your strengths and abilities. Your post is so much greater than all of these limitations. Your post is what most would simply call, "Your Destiny."

Terry Smith in his book, *Ten*, describes our destiny like this, "it's the pre-destined context of our lives." This basically means, before the foundations of the earth, before the spirit of God was hovering across the waters, before He blew His breath into a body that He created out of the dust of the ground, He had your destiny in mind. He knew who he created you to be and how you were going to fit into His kingdom's tapestry.

"Crazy, right?" Before the foundations of the world, He had you in his heart. See, it is that destiny, the pre-destined context from which we live our lives, that I am going to call Your Post!

Much like the Watchman on the Wall in Scripture, your post is a "military type" position. The watchman had a distinct post which included a position and an assignment. Picture with me an old citadel with a city courtyard much like you would see on medieval movie sets. Towers protrude up past the wall and a guard is stationed on top, the watchman. He was strategically positioned there to protect the city. Behind him stands the fortress he is protecting. In front of him are people coming and going in and out of the citadel. Some enemies, some friends; some merchants, some leaders.

The watchman's job is to discern who and what is coming in and how it's going to affect the city. He has a post, a military position. It is both offensive and defensive.

Much like this watchman, our post is a military watch, a calling for which we are responsible. We are to know the kingdom context of our lives: what God has created, designed and pre-destined us to do -- positioned to know what is coming and to see how it is going to affect and move within the context of what He has called us to do.

Our Post is not to be confused with purpose. People tend to flounder in life, lost from "purpose to purpose to purpose." You see, purpose is not destiny. We have used the terms interchangeably, but let's distinguish the two. Purpose is seasonal. It is based around the seasons in our life which will change.

Many marriages go through an empty nest time that can be very difficult. That is where marriages can fail. Arguments happen. There is difficulty relating and connecting to each other on a new level. It is because their identity got wrapped up in a seasonal purpose.

Seasonal purpose would relate to the ever-changing roles of a mother throughout her children's life, from the mother of an infant, to toddler, to the early years of elementary school, high school, college, becoming a mother-in-law, a grandmother, a great-grandmother. Her roles change throughout the course of her child's life--seasonal purpose. This may also relate to changing careers, economic conditions, or family and friendships that change over the years. All of these areas and endless others represent seasonal purpose. In our lives, the enemy traps us into believing that our identity is attached to this seasonal purpose. We are not defined by the seasons in our lives; we are defined by the Creator Himself. Our identity is in Him and is being formed by Him.

What we are talking about is NOT seasonal purpose. We are talking about your identity, your destiny, your post in the kingdom of God. Your purpose within the context of this post is going to change from season to season. It is going to change and grow, just like children grow up and change. It is going to change just like jobs change, industry changes, or the economy changes. Your purpose from season to season is going to change. What God has called you to actually do in these seasons is going to change. But the life that infuses that destiny, the kingdom context of your life does not change! What we must discover is that place of destiny, our post, so that everything we do in the various seasonal purposes in our lives flows from this context.

There is a Divine umbrella over your life that is your post, your destiny. It is a high positional calling! God had it in His mind before the foundation of the earth! Within the context of that huge umbrella, is seasonal purpose. You'll have many assignments throughout the course of your life. Your jobs may change. Your responsibilities, friendships, and ministry opportunities will change. Seasonal purpose changes, but your identity does not budge, because it is Kingdom birthed!

"This is powerful stuff!" Our post is not a title or an occupation, nor is it something others proclaim about you. It is not given by man because it is so much bigger. Titles and positions within your occupation are attached to seasonal purpose, not to identity. Who you are is not based on what other people call you or how high up on the corporate ladder you ascend. Who you are has nothing to do with what you are doing in your life. Who you are is based on God's divine nature placed inside of you and His Kingdom-agenda for your life. It's your Post!

We don't choose our post, but we do choose whether or not we are going to command that post. In order to command that post, we need to understand the 3 "P's " of our Post: Position, Passion and Posture.

**Know your Position**
**Identify your Passion**
**and Strengthen your Posture.**

## *Chapter 24*

# POSITION

### COMMANDING YOUR POST IS REALIZED
### BY
### FINDING & MAINTAINING YOUR POSITION

Before we can partner with God and fulfill our individual destinies, we need to discover what the Kingdom boundaries are of our lives. What is your destined place? For most, this post is not necessarily a geographical location but a spiritual position. Now my father, Bishop Tommy Reid, actually has a geographical location that directly coincides with his post because he is an apostle by nature, but the entirety of his post exceeds that location. For most of us, however, a geographical location probably does not define our post. A post is something that is much more spiritual and philosophical. It is something that is directly tied to your spiritual DNA, who you are, and how you are called to function in life.

We need to personally define this post so that we can "own it." The simplest way to begin is to ask the Lord, "What am I here for?" You are never too young or too old to ask that question. You've never come too far, nor are you ever too lost to ask it. Just like hitting the reboot on a computer when it is all seized up, reboot...ask the question, what am I here for?

Once we know this, we can pursue our post and find what I call, "the sweet spot of living!" It is a divine, beautiful place. This does not mean that the current of our lives always flows peacefully all of the time. It certainly does not mean that the enemy ceases his attack or that things do not fall apart. Yet, it is a sweet spot because you live feeling fulfilled because you are in your kingdom zone. The only time that you are ever truly fulfilled is when you're living within the context of your post. Sometimes we get so caught up in seasonal purposes and the things that we desire to do, that we zig-zag all over the roadmaps of our lives.

One minute we are here, the next minute we're there. We fail to realize that our post does not change. As your understanding of it matures, it enlarges but does not change-- like the prayer of Jabez, "enlarge my territory." The territory of your post grows because you mature in your understanding of it throughout your life. The way God created you, the way He formed you, and what He destined for your life never changes.

So what is that specific sweet spot for your life? If you're not functioning in that sweet spot, you still may have times where you will feel good about your life as things are going well and feel satisfying.

Don't mistake temporary satisfaction with fulfillment because they are two totally different things. Just like sin is temporarily satisfying, there's nothing as fulfilling as walking in covenant with God. Our post is a reflection of this same covenant and brings true fulfillment to our lives.

Knowing our post gives us the framework to make every decision in our lives. We determine all things in light of our post, not what is going to make more money, not even what is going to provide our families with a better life. In living our lives in the center of God's will, He covers all our needs in an extraordinary way. Once we understand this post and flip our motivations, we are free to claim some pretty outlandish covenant promises. Think about it:  what business do we have claiming the promises of God when we are consistently living outside of His will for our lives? His promises are made to be fulfilled when we're functioning in the sphere where God's called us to live. Get the big picture! It is a Kingdom appointment. That does not mean that God's not going to touch you outside of that sphere, but within that post, you can go ahead and dig into His Word and claim those incredible covenant promises. They are directly tied to your post, so they are yours to claim!

What is the specific position God has in His heart for you? To better understand it, let's look at the 3 "D's" of this position: God dreamed it. God defined it. And God promises to disclose it to you.

## God-Dreamed
## — it was birthed in the dreams of God

He dreamed you into existence! It was from His imagination; it was from His creativity that He designed you. It began in His heart, way before the time you were born, before the foundations of the world, God dreamed your post! He dreamed you!

Ps. 139 says it best ...
Vs 13 "For you created my inmost being;

You knit me together in my mothers womb."

Vs 16 "All the days ordained for me were written in your
book before one of them came to be."

God dreamed the very thing that He created and designed you for, and wrote it in His book even before you ever breathed your first breath! It is in your DNA!

We have a specific part in His dream, a Kingdom-agenda dream. It's about spreading His Kingdom and enlarging His influence upon the face of the earth -- reaching with His super-natural power through us to a lost and dying world. That is His dream! His dream is manifold — multi-dimensional, endless dimensions that manifold. Biblically, this term is used in the context in describing the rainbow, having manifold colors. Not just made up like a child's drawing of six colors, the rainbow is infinite in its color combinations.

God has a manifold plan-agenda for all of the earth, it's endless. All of us have a specific role in that plan, in fact, you're one of the manifold colors. Think about it like a great painting. You have an extraordinarily specific color, a specific width, depth, height of the stroke of God's paintbrush. Without you, there is a blank place on the canvas and His plan is incomplete. God's Dream is a manifold dream in which you have a position to discover!

## God-Defined
## — it is a fixed position determined by God

### Acts 17:26-28 (Amplified)

*And He made from one [common origin, one source, one blood] all nations of men to settle on the face of the earth, having definitely determined [their] allotted periods of time and the fixed boundaries of their habitation (their settlements, lands, and abodes). So that they should seek God, in the hope that they might seek after Him and find Him, although He is not far from each one of us. For in Him we live and move and have our being.*

In this profound scripture, John is speaking of God's intended plan for the lives of people, the crowning glory of His creation. He made us from one common origin, from His very breath, to live a life of supernatural union with Him, within the context of divine, fixed boundaries.

There is a fixed place where we are called to seamlessly move in Him and He in us. It is definitively fixed. It is not up to us to decide the size or location of that place. Our track record is marred by catastrophes. Haven't we been deciding these things long enough? Let us turn the boundaries of our habitation over to the dreams of God.

Since this post is a position that God-dreamed, it is also a position of living that God defines. It has parameters. It has boundary markers that are specific and permanent.

Joshua 1:2-6 NIV reads, "Moses my servant is dead. Now then, you and all these people, get ready to cross the Jordan River into the land I am about to give to them–to the Israelites. I will give you every place where you set your foot, as I promised Moses. Your territory will extend from the desert to Lebanon, and from the great river, the Euphrates–all the Hittite country– to the Great Sea on the west. No one will be able to stand up against you all the days of your life. As I was with Moses, so I will be with you; I will never leave you nor forsake you. Be strong and courageous, because you will lead these people to inherit the land I swore to their forefathers to give them."

When Moses died, God spoke to Joshua and said that He was going to give him every piece of ground that he would stand on. The Lord then goes on to define the ground with boundary markings. He did not just say to Joshua, I am going to give every piece so that you can run around all over the planet and say, "this ground is mine, and this ground is mine." It was a specific promise; there were definitive boundaries attached to the promise. He basically was saying to Joshua, "Here is your post, look at this specific property. You are to raise up a generation and lead them to inherit this land which I will give to you." That was his post. It was defined, and it had parameters. Within those parameters, Joshua would know that He could be strong and courageous because God would never leave Him and therefore, anything would be possible!

Just like the promise given to Joshua, our post in life also has definitive parameters, and within that context, all things are possible! What are those boundaries? First of all, our post has moral parameters. That's a commonality for all of us.

While mainstream, modern Christianity would try to deny it, we do live by a system of absolutes. This system of absolutes provides protection, power, and integrity in the life of the believer. We follow Him in integrity because we love Him and do not want to hurt our relationship with anything that would divide our heart from walking in perfect harmony with Him! The most fantastic part is that His grace pours over us to empower us to walk it out! Jesus died, we embrace Him as Savior, and we become righteous. Period. Now He showers us with His grace, and we can live out of His righteousness, walking in integrity, living a lifestyle of worship, honoring this indescribable finished work!

In finding and maintaining this post positionally, you will continually flounder if you do not strive to live within the moral boundaries that God has designed. You will feed your flesh rather than the spirit. You will lose sight of God's destiny for your life and live a life sub-standard to what God has called you to live. That goes for morality, attitudes, how you speak, treat others, show love and extend grace. See, we are called to live within morally and ethically defined parameters. If you are going to live in that defined territory, you cannot act unethically in business and relationships or you are going to misuse your post and gray out its boundaries. And, "there goes the neighborhood!"

Secondly, your post has territorial parameters. God does not want you trying to be someone else. He has a specific post for you. I'm not an athlete as much as I would like to be. My husband will tell you that when I try to run, I look like a flamingo tumbling on the beach. If I tried to go out and pursue sports and said, "I can do all things through Jesus Christ who gives me strength," well, let's just say I wouldn't get very far. I could name it and claim it all I want, but if it's not within the context of the territorial parameters God has dreamed for my life, it will not come to pass. Now, supply a piano and say, "Aimee, lead these people in worship, take them into an encounter with the glory of God," now I can declare, "I can do all things through Christ Jesus" because I am well within the territorial parameters God has destined for my life! It's the sweet spot where I was born to live!

The amazing thing about these territorial parameters is that they are so very much larger than you could ever imagine! God sees more for your life than you could ever dream up so why try to define this position for yourself any longer? It is ALL about living in that place, and God giving us exactly what we need--every talent, ability, power and grace to live in that perfectly-defined place. Life should be spent, finding and living within the parameters of your post and oh, the beautiful satisfaction, personal fulfillment, and supernatural provision that will come!

## God-Disclosed
## — one that God desires to reveal to us

The position of your post is God-dreamed. It is God-defined, and it is God-disclosed to us! God desires to reveal it to us. We do not wander aimlessly searching for it. He walks with us and whispers these beautiful secrets in our ear out of a love relationship.

**I Corinthians 2:9, 10 & 16 (Amplified)**

*"...as the Scripture says, What eye has not seen and ear has not heard and has not entered into the heart of man, [all that] God has prepared (made and keeps ready) for those who love Him [who hold Him in affectionate reverence, promptly obeying Him and gratefully recognizing the benefits He has bestowed]. Yet to us God has unveiled and revealed them by and through His Spirit, for the [Holy] Spirit searches diligently, exploring and examining everything, even sounding the profound and bottomless things of God [the divine counsels and things hidden and beyond man's scrutiny] ... For who has known or understood the mind (the counsels and purposes) of the Lord so as to guide and instruct Him and give Him knowledge? But we have the mind of Christ (the Messiah) and do hold the thoughts (feelings and purposes) of His heart."*

Your post is one of the deep mysteries of God. Some people spend their lives trying to figure this out intellectually when God says that by His Spirit, it will be revealed. Your post in life is a spiritual matter. It's your spiritual territory that has natural ramifications. God reveals spiritual things by the power of His Spirit, not by the power of intellect. It is a spiritual matter that requires a relationship with the Holy Spirit who dwells in you.

Through this relationship, it will translate into your intellect so you will know what to do with the operations of your life.

Jesus spoke of this to His disciples in John 16:7 "... *I am telling you nothing but the truth when I say it is profitable (good, expedient, advantageous) for you that I go away. Because if I do not go away, the Comforter (Counselor, Helper, Advocate, Intercessor, Strengthener, Standby) will not come to you [into close fellowship with you]; but if I go away, I will send Him to you [to be in close fellowship with you].*" Amplified Version

Christ goes on to say in verses 12-15, "*I have still many things to say to you, but you are not able to bear them or to take them upon you or to grasp them now. But when He, the Spirit of Truth (the Truth- giving Spirit) comes, He will guide you into all the Truth (the whole, full Truth). For He will not speak His own message [on His own authority]; but He will tell whatever He hears [from the Father; He will give the message that has been given to Him], and He will announce and declare to you the things that are to come [that will happen in the future]. He will honor and glorify Me, because He will take of (receive, draw upon) what is Mine and will reveal (declare, disclose, transmit) it to you. Everything that the Father has is Mine. That is what I meant when I said that He [the Spirit] will take the things that are Mine and will reveal (declare, disclose, transmit) it to you.*" (Amplified Version)

This passage is filled with revelation for us. Jesus is about to walk out His earthly destiny on the cross. His physical presence is leaving the disciples. It is so hard to imagine-- Jesus Himself, walking in close relationship with them, being physically present among them. Now, He's leaving and as life-altering as this was going to be for the disciples, Jesus candidly says this is the best thing that could happen to them! Wow! This is how much Jesus believed in the ministry of the Holy Spirit. It is meant to be even "better" than having Jesus personally present with us. This blows my mind!

He promises that what was about to come was going to reveal TRUTH, truth that comes directly from the eternal realm. This Holy Spirit has access to everything that is of Christ. He draws upon it and then reveals it to man. It would be as if Christ was still with them, but not limited to one location and one group of people, dwelling now within each life. The Holy Spirit will take the things of Christ, truth and revelation regarding all things, and disclose it to those who are filled with His Spirit.

So, Christ is then crucified, declares the finished work, dies, rises again in the perfection of resurrection power, and then begins to make various appearances among the people before ascending to take His ultimate place in the power seat of the universe! In one of His appearances, He comes to the disciples in John 20:19-20: *"Then on that same first day of the week, when it was evening, though the disciples were behind closed doors for fear of the Jews, Jesus came and stood among them and said, 'Peace to you!' So saying, He showed them His hands and His side. And when the disciples saw the Lord, they were filled with joy (delight, exultation, ecstasy, rapture). Then Jesus said to them again, Peace to you! [Just] as the Father has sent Me forth, so I am sending you. And having said this, He breathed on them and said to them, Receive the Holy Spirit!"* Amplified Version

The Holy Spirit is the tangible breath of the Godhead. The Holy Spirit, never bound to the limitations of a physical body, completely Divine, was given to man this day. This Spirit is the invisible, yet tangible breath of God in our lives. This breath speaks, it motivates, heals, empowers, guides, comforts, renews, restores, and re-defines our lives. Perhaps we have relegated the Holy Spirit to such an intangible, mystical role that we have missed the tangible dimension of a personal relationship with Him!

Jesus breathed into man, giving us His Spirit which reveals His heart and mysteries to us. Your post is the mystery of God's will disclosed. The Holy Spirit will disclose it to you. He will reveal it to you, He will transmit it to you. Before time began, God had a great secret about your life. It was your destiny, your post. It is humanly incomprehensible. God uses the weak things of this world to confound the strong and the foolish things to "mess up the wise ones" (1 Corinthians 1:27). Your post is spiritually destined and because it is spiritually destined, it goes beyond your imagination; beyond all natural possibilities. It is yours to grab hold of through a vibrant relationship with the Holy Spirit!

The position of your post is apprehended by the understanding that God dreamed it, God defines it, and God wills to disclose it to you.

## Spiritual Positioning

Within the positional parameters of our post, our lives reach an apex of true fulfillment. Pause for a moment and honestly search within yourself. Are you living the abundant life that Jesus came to bring you (John 10:10)?

The key to walking in this abundant life is finding out the parameters of your walk. Some are moral, some are ethical, philosophical, Biblical—perhaps all of these. It is a spiritual territory that we are called to command for our entire life.

A spiritual position is accompanied by spiritual blessings.

It brings fulfillment, a life of abundant provision, covenant promises and decrees over your life. Within this position, is power for life-long endurance and realization of the anointing of the Holy Spirit. We were born for this post. We were created for it! Outside of these parameters, come unnecessary difficulties, strain, and confusion that are sub-standard living in the kingdom of God.

I've heard it said that, "You are a spiritual being having an earthly experience." Outside of Divinely determined parameters, we struggle. I'm sure we can all say today, "Yes, I walked in both lanes. When I lived outside of the will of God for my life, I struggled unnecessarily. Once I got back in the zone of where I was called to be and what I am called to do, things changed." Right?

It doesn't mean that struggles disappeared, but that your endurance levels increased. Your understanding and your awareness of your struggles were different. They might look the same, but your struggles are producing something now. You are growing and life is accelerating in fruitfulness. But outside of these parameters is a struggle for nothing. In Kingdom context, our earthly experience will not always be easy, but every difficulty produces Kingdom harvest and we, as spiritual beings, grow in strength and impact.

So how do we find this position? If it's a spiritual position with spiritual blessings, then there's a spiritual answer to this question. Let us begin with the foundational initiative: develop daily secured times of prayer and devotion to nurture our relationship with the Lord. It is vital for us to secure a block of time every day to be with our Maker, the Lover of my soul--to be with Jesus and commune with the Holy Spirit. We must make a determination to keep this time secure. If this time is random, so is your position. When it is secured, things change. A secured times of prayer births new levels of worship—communion with God. It opens up the eyes of our understanding to the revelation of Him and what He has called us to do. Without it, there's confusion. It also sensitizes us to the voice of God, so we can hear and truly know His leading and direction.

In Ephesians 1:17-18, Paul reveals his heart for the church at Ephesus by saying, *"[For I always pray to] the God of our Lord Jesus Christ, the Father of glory, that He may grant you a spirit of wisdom and revelation [of insight into mysteries and secrets] in the [deep and intimate] knowledge of Him, by having the eyes of your heart flooded with light, so that you can know and understand the hope to which He has called you, and how rich is His glorious inheritance in the saints (His set-apart ones)."* Amplified Version

Finding our position comes from having the eyes of our heart enlightened by a relationship with the Holy Spirit. It is not head knowledge that we have rationalized. Head knowledge will cancel out heart understanding and ultimately will cancel out your position. As soon as you try to rationalize something, you will diminish it. If you are trying to rationalize what God has called you to do, you will never put your foot to it because you are going to try to alter it and make it sensical. You will start taking the fact that "His ways are higher than your ways" and flip it by putting your head-knowledge on top of His ways. In matters of revelation, you have got to let go of your thinker and start trusting your heart. Remember though that the only way you can trust your heart is through these dedicated times of prayer and worship. Your heart is trustworthy when it is submitted to the Holy Spirit on a daily basis.

What color of God's manifold kingdom rainbow are you? What is the width, depth, and height of the stroke of God's paintbrush which you are on His beautiful canvas? God's Dream is a manifold dream in which you have a position to discover--the position of Your Post!

## *Chapter 25*

# PASSION

## COMMANDING YOUR POST IS REALIZED
## BY
## THE DISCOVERY OF YOUR PASSIONS

*"Christianity was never to be known for its disciplines;*
*it was to be known by its passions."*
**Bill Johnson**
*Hosting the Presence: Unveiling Heaven's Agenda*

This is revelation for the Body of Christ. Think about it. How many people in the world are offended by Christianity because all they see is what we stand against? Should not Christianity be known by what we are for and not by what we are against? We are to be known by the love and destiny that drives us.

This is Passion: what motivates us, drives us, and compels us. Godly passion comes from within and was placed in our very DNA by our creator. It drives us to pursue Him, motivates us to accomplish His purposes, and compels us to participate in that which is in His heart! Passion comes from an experiential reality of God that is not based on head knowledge but on heart connection. When you have a true heart connection with God, you have passion. There is divine energy that is put inside of you to do and to accomplish the things that are on His heart.

The burdens on the heart of God are not an easy thing to bear. Over the course of the last few years, God has burned His passion for the children of the world into my heart, particularly the children that are the victims of child sex trafficking and slavery. It has gone beyond an issue that disturbs me and has become the driving force of this particular season of my life. In prayer I have seen horrific visions of children taken into this bondage. I have seen their faces and bruises, and felt a dimension of their suffering that has wrecked me. It has moved me so deeply that I cannot let it go! I am willing to risk it all for the sake of the children. His passion has become my passion. And so, a revelation of a new purpose within my post is emerging.

Passion that is Godly takes what is on His heart and infuses it into our hearts. God's passion is what He feels in His heart. Your passions are to be defined by His passions. God gives us these passions to help us connect with His kingdom reality and define our post.

We should all have common passions: our love for God, our love for worship, and perhaps above all, our love for people. These common passions should define the body of Christ! Yet there are passions that are unique to each one of us.

In my life, the larger reality of my post is that I am called to guard and protect the image and presence of God within the territory God has ordained for my life. I am a guardian. That is quite evident at my home ministry, The Tabernacle of Orchard Park, NY. I'm like a bulldog at the door if someone wants to come in and mess with the atmosphere. I am on my watchtower guarding how we handle the Presence of God and the flow of the river among us. There is also the other side of my post where I am charged to protect the image of God. To me that translates as protecting and enlarging how He is seen. The world may see Him as a judge on a bench, but He is truly the one and only King on the throne. He is a God of grace and mercy who is worthy to be worshipped and adored. Yet, He is a God of Justice who causes us to stand in awe! Therefore, I preach, teach, pastor, minister and am a lead worshipper forging the way for others to discover the presence and dimensions of the knowledge of the Glory of God in their lives.

This discovery of my post has emerged out of my passions. Throughout my life, I have always had a passion for music. I immersed myself in music of all styles from classical to jazz, rock to R&B. I practiced piano for hours on end. Studied classical pieces and their interpretations by various pianists. I would digest musical charts and then practice until I just couldn't play another note! Melodies, rhythmic patterns, and lyrics would fill my head all day and night. This passion compelled me and brought much enjoyment to my life. As I followed this passion for music over the years, my post began to emerge. I played professionally in different venues, but my post became undeniable. Worship music brought people into dimensions of the presence of God that healed them, restored them, transformed lives forever. Nothing else in music could do this! The vehicle was my passion for music, but the ultimate destination was a deep love for leading people into worship. My GPS has locked in on the territory of my post!

Following after our God-given passions also aides the equipping process in our lives. My passion for music equipped me with a proficiency I use every day in my post. God places seeds of talent in our lives, and it is up to us to develop these seeds into abilities. We also go through seasons of purpose that equip us for what we will need to be able to do in the future. You may think you are in a meaningless season right now, but just maybe God will use what you are doing now to equip you for greater things to come! Wouldn't that be just like Him?

The identification and discovery of God's passion in our lives enable us to discover our posts. He intricately designed you with that passion so that you will be compelled to go after all that He has for you. Your passions are directly tied to your post. Because your post utilizes your passions, it brings fulfillment and satisfaction to your life that is astounding. You are never too old to figure out what your passions are, and you are certainly never too young either. Why waste another day living outside of your God-given passions? Identify them and the revelation of your post will not be far behind!

## Divine Passion

Passion was put in our lives because He is a passionate God. Passion is what compelled Him to the cross. That's why it is called the Passion of Christ. It compelled Him to go where no one else could have gone so that you would be free! Passion is Godly, it comes from Him and is put in your life to help you define and empower your post. The discovery of Divine passion comes from the pursuit of a living relational experience with God. We pursue Him because He went the extra mile to pursue us. He found us when we were lost and dying, and brought us to life. He pursued us, and now we pursue Him.

In *When Heaven Invades Earth*, Bill Johnson states, "Biblical passion is a mysterious mixture of humility, supernatural hunger, and faith. I pursue because I have been pursued." This divine passion is a deep well inside each one of us. We tap into this well when we humble ourselves, admitting we cannot even breathe without Him, that we are totally reliant on Him in every way. As we pursue after Him, our hunger continues to increase ... the more we find Him, the more we long for Him. It is a beautiful cycle of continuous encounter! Faith then increases as we find the personal presence of God in our lives. His tangibility becomes so present, that we become absolutely certain of who He is and what He will do as we step out in Him! Humility, hunger, and faith--the ingredients of Divine passion.

David expressed this Divine passion perfectly in Psalm 63:8: *"My whole being follows hard after You and clings closely to You; Your right hand upholds me."* (Amplified Version) Perhaps this is why the Lord characterized David as a "man after His own heart" (1 Samuel 13:14 / Acts 13:21). Was it because David always walked in personal integrity and purity? Certainly not. I read that passage quite literally, David was a man who pursued after the heart of God. He walked in humility, hunger, and faith. His deep well of passion drove him to worship God without inhibitions. This passion for God defined David's life, and ultimately led Him to the discovery of His post. His seasonal purpose as King, did not define His post. David's passion for the presence of God drove Him to build a pattern of worship that is still on God's agenda to restore (Acts 15:16-17)! His post could be defined as a keeper of the flame, a lead worshipper who was a guardian of the glory of God. Even in his death, David's post is still at work.

I love how the the Message Bible reads in Mark 12:30: Jesus commanded them, "so love the Lord God with all your passion and prayer and intelligence and energy...." These qualities embody those who live in a passionate relationship with God. There is absolutely nothing like Godly passion! The enemy tries to pervert passion and equate it to sexual desires. This is his trap, once he entangles us, this desire becomes fierce and can never be satisfied. How do you explain aged men destroying innocent children in this way? When we misinterpret passion as sexual desire, it has no fulfillment. It is just not possible because nothing ever fully satisfies. So the enemy has entrapped generations of people with filth and such erotic nonsense that rages so fiercely that now the lions are consuming goldfish trying to quench the fire within.

Passion was put in to you by your Creator, and it cannot be fulfilled by earthly things. Your passions cannot even be fully met inside the context of a Godly marriage because it is not just about your flesh or your soul, it is about your spirit. Passions can only be fully expressed, fully realized, and fully met in your relationship with Jesus. Your marriage then becomes an outflow of the divine and divine intimacy increases the beauty of the marriage in all dimensions. In kingdom context, passion is not fleshly desire. Passion was placed in you by the Creator! When you are able to live out of your passions, you live fulfilled, destined, anointed and empowered lives.

The identification and discovery of your unique Godly passions enables you to define your post. Your post and your passion in the Kingdom are perfectly intertwined together. God put those specific passions in your life to first of all, be met in Him; secondly, to do all the things that are inside of you to do. Whether it's art or music, showing love to people, taking care of babies, organizing, developing budgets, ministering to hurting people, handing out food or helping others put their lives together--whatever it is, it is directly tied to your post. You are designed that way for a greater destiny. Can you see now why fulfillment increases when you are living life inside the boundaries of your post? Even when the hard times come our way and life becomes more difficult, it can be powerfully navigated because your passions are being utilized and expressed in the Kingdom context of your post.

**Philippians 2:12 (Message Bible)**
*"What I'm getting at, friends, is that you should simply keep on doing what you have done from the beginning. When I was living among you, you lived in responsive obedience. Now that I am separated from you, keep it up. Better yet, redouble your efforts. Be energetic in your life of salvation, reverent and sensitive before God. 13 That energy (PASSION) is God's energy (PASSION), an energy deep within you, God himself willing and working at what will give him the most pleasure. (emphasis mine)*

The most beautiful thing about living from His divine passions inside of us is not that we live more fulfilled lives, it is that He receives pleasure. Have you ever thought, "God, I could never repay You for all You have done in my life!" Well, you actually can! You can give Him the greatest gift-- you! Allow Him to live His passions through you. You are His living body on the earth. We are His arms extended, His heart revealed in the world. He takes such pleasure in relationship with us. He loves when we fully express our passions to Him. Such pleasure He receives when we allow Him to satisfy our innermost passions! He made you for Himself, to enjoy you, to intimately commune with you, and through that, to fulfill His Kingdom agenda in partnership with you! Discover the purity of His Divine passions in you, and you find your post!

*Chapter 26*

# Posture

## Commanding Your Post Is Realized By Strengthening Your Posture

**Ephesians 6:11**

*"Put on God's whole armor [the armor of a heavy-armed soldier which God supplies], that you may be able successfully to stand up against [all] the strategies and the deceits of the devil."* *(Amplified Version)*

## "Able"

Two words you must own in this passage: "able" and "stand." The word able in this scripture comes from the same Greek word which means Power (dunamis), which is a dynamic power. It actually describes the explosive ability and dynamic strength we have when we are equipped with the whole armor of God. We have explosive and dynamic power at our command! The armor of God, when properly worn and utilized, makes us able to stand with explosive power for living. It equips us to confront the enemy both offensively and defensively.

Your post is a territory designed by God for you. If you do not take it, the enemy will! Maybe he already has, and it is time for you to reclaim it. The enemy has acted as if he is the Lord of this world, but we know his end and we know the only one that is truly Lord, that is Jesus Christ the King! We must participate and enforce this victory with the dynamic power that makes us able. Jesus IS going to have the final victory, and He is going to do it through an army that has taken the territory we are called to take.

That term "dynamic" is interesting as well. I think of dynamics from a musical perspective. It is how one note relates to another. The beauty of music depends on dynamics. If a piece has little dynamics it is uninteresting and has little impact. On the other hand, if a piece has many highs and lows in volume and tonality, along with a variety in melodic structure and rhythmic patterns, it can be very beautiful and have great impact on the listener. This is the dynamic force of music.

A great friend and co-lead worshipper at my home ministry, The Tabernacle, is also a high-school science teacher who describes this term, dynamic, scientifically as "a force having to do with..." whatever they are discussing in class. A dictionary would use terms like "the science of moving powers," the power one force exerts on another.

A great example is in the human body. Homeostasis is when the body is in dynamic equilibrium. The body will continually adjust itself to maintain this dynamic equilibrium. This could be as simple as when fighting an illness your body adjusts its temperature, or when you are hungry your body tells your brain that you need food. There is a dynamic force that God instituted in man to keep us healthy and alive. Gravity is also a dynamic force. We see and feel the affects of gravity, but no one can fully comprehend its source. All scientists know that because of gravity all bodies have a dynamic affect on each other. There is a law in physics called the Inverse Square Law that states when the distance between two objects is halved, the gravitational attraction (dynamics) between them quadruples. This all has incredible significance when it comes to our spiritual life. We are called to maintain a spiritual dynamic equilibrium. When we feel cold, discouraged, or far away from the Lord ,we need to tap into the realm of worship to come back into dynamic equilibrium. His presence has a dynamic impact on our soul (our mind, will and emotions). In His presence, we come back into the balance of the Spirit and realize the dynamic that makes us able to live an extraordinary life. Our Spirit is like gravity, if we can just halve the distance between us and the eternal realm, the force between us quadruples and we begin to feel the dynamic explosive power of the Spirit in our lives, dunamis power. From our lives flows a beautiful dynamic song that has great impact for the Kingdom of God!

## "To Stand"

We are able, we have the dunamis power, the dynamic strength and explosive ability, that causes us to stand against all the strategies and deceits of the enemy. "To stand" in the original Greek language means to make to stand, to be confirmed, established, fixed, to hold upright, weighted. It is the image of a proud and confident soldier, not one who is slumped over in defeat and despondency.

I have had the honor to meet many American soldiers who have been wounded on the battlefield with life-altering injuries. Men and women in their early twenties who are left without legs, arms, or any combinations of both outward and inward injuries. Yet, these soldiers were not slumped over in defeat and despondency. Even through their associated emotional battles from PTSD, I am telling you that there was still something in their eyes. There was an incomprehensible strength inside of them that said, "No defeat!" This is the perfect picture of the dunamis power to stand that each one of us has by the Spirit of God!

We have a responsibility to stand confirmed, established, fixed and upright in the power of God with the whole armor on. This is how we strengthen our posture. We daily pick-up each piece of armor and fix it to our spiritual man! Grab the ornate helmet of salvation that intricately reaches to every element of your past and redeems it, that appropriates every provision of the cross upon us, and that guards our mind in Christ Jesus! Affix the shiny, glamorous breastplate of righteousness stating that you are and have been made righteous in Christ Jesus. Just the reflection of the light of God's glory on this shiny piece of armor will blind and confuse the enemy! Take up the huge shield of faith, the size of a door, that protects us and quenches the "fiery darts" of the enemy. Buckle the belt of truth around your waist, the whole written word of God (the logos word - the book from cover to cover), that fastens the other pieces of armor together. From the belt of truth, draw the sword of the spirit which is the rhema Word of God (the revelation word that comes alive from the written word, and is used to assault the enemy at close range). Strap on the shoes of peace from toe to kneecap. These are killer shoes! Shoes with three inch spikes both underneath and protruding from the toe. These shoes not only cause us to stand firmly in place regardless of the condition of the ground, but they take down the enemy with one kick and enable us to just walk straight on over him, mutilating him. The enemy is truly under your feet (Psalm 8:6); now just keep advancing and walk over him with those killer shoes! Finally, the last weapon is one Paul does not mention but one that a Roman soldier would have carried, the lance. This was their long-range weapon they would wield to take out the enemy coming in from the distance. Are you tired of feeling like you are always in a close range battle with the enemy? Well, take up your lance of prayer and worship, and with the eyes of the spirit, take him out at long range! Put on this armor carefully and deliberately each day. It's the posture of your post!

## Strengthen Your Posture

Picture with me a young boy trying to put on a suit of armor. If he is strong enough to actually pick up each piece and put it on, would he be strong enough to move in this heavy suit and actually utilize each piece of weaponry? Chances are, many of us have this same problem with the armor of God. Our muscles and posture is too weak to handle the weight of the armor, let alone utilize it effectively. Our posture needs to be strengthened in order to be able to function victoriously in our post. There is a battle waging against us, and this battle is not just outward against the enemy, but it is inward as well. Our greatest enemy may even be ourselves.

## Re-Orient

We strengthen our posture by, first of all, reorienting ourselves. Notice here: I am intentionally implying that we are disoriented. Have you ever been through a physical sickness, coming in and out of a fever or migraine headache, and felt like the world is spinning around you, not knowing quite where you are or what is happening? This is a great example of how many of us function in our lives. We feel lost in a spinning world, purposeless and powerless--disoriented. Perhaps because the enemy has hit, or something is constantly distracting and overwhelming us, we are left feeling weak and disabled. As hard as it is to let go of all the distractions and heavy burdens, we have to intentionally reorient ourselves and get back into position.

The Oxford Dictionary defines "reorient" as a verb meaning to change the focus or direction of, to find one's position again in relation to one's surroundings. Other dictionaries describe this word as "to set or arrange in a different, determinate position." In our lives, we struggle during seasons to maintain our focus when our surroundings change or hard times come. To reorient ourself is to find our position and focus again, even when circumstances are reluctant to change. Determination has to grip us--not to settle for defeat, blurred focus, passivity, or mediocrity any longer. We must reorient ourselves when we feel disoriented and rise up to command our post. Strengthening our posture requires this determined decision.

## Re-Equip

Nurturing our relationship with God on a daily basis is our most important goal. Rick Renner in his book, *Dressed to Kill*, communicates an important truth about Paul's instruction in Ephesians 6:11: "The armor of God is ours by virtue of our relationship with God!" He (Paul) wanted us to know that this armor originates in God and is freely bestowed upon those who continually draw their life and their existence from God. Your unbroken, ongoing fellowship with God is your absolute guarantee that you are constantly and habitually dressed in the whole armor of God."

We cannot rely on "yesterday's revelation" to carry us into tomorrow. God is always speaking and continuously on the move. If we are stagnant or stuck in yesterday, then it appears as if He is moving away from or not speaking to us. This is just not the case. Correct perspective remains that He is moving and unless we keep moving with Him, it will appear as if He is moving far from us when in reality the burden of distance remains on us. We must stay in immediate proximity of His presence in order to tune in to His voice and keep moving with Him.

In Psalm 105:3-4, the Psalmist employs, *"Glory in His holy name; let the hearts of those rejoice who seek and require the Lord [as their indispensable necessity]. Seek, inquire of the Lord, and crave Him and His strength (His might and inflexibility to temptation); seek and require His face and His presence [continually] evermore."* (Amplified Version)

We must tend to the presence of God in our lives, living for relationship with Him. I love how the Amplified Bible reads in this passage that we are to seek Him as our "indispensable necessity." "Crave Him. . .seek and require His face and His presence continually." There is a depth of urgency and complete reliance communicated with this wording. It speaks to our motivation. Do you live for His hand to move in your life, or do you live for His heart?

His presence is everything! Tending to His presence is living a lifestyle that continuously pursues His face, and rearranges everything in your life to accommodate more and more of Him. No distraction or temptation is worth displacing His presence.

The re-equipping process begins with tending to His

presence in our lives, daily drawing all our life and existence from Him. As we do so, we gain new revelation and power to not only dress in the full armor of God, but to utilize it in strengthening the posture of our Post!

## Re-Align

Proper alignment is critical in most aspects of our life. I think of alignment in three primary ways. First of all, the term alliances; our relational alignments are of utmost importance. Who do stand aligned with, to relate to, trust, value, respect, and honor? Are there spiritual mentors in your life, friendships who balance you, and people that hold you accountable? Do you connect predominantly with those who edify you, or those who bring you down? Consider carefully whom the Lord has sent into your life as an alignment for your life.

The second way I view the term alignment is in setting things in order. The ability to prioritize, order, adjust, and unify things in life is priceless. Confusion and disarray render us ineffective. Are there areas of your life that do not line up with the Kingdom? Do you live life randomly or deliberately in accordance with a Godly plan? Can you easily submit your will and desires to the Lord? Have the courage to ask Him today to order your life in alignment with His priorities and purposes. It can be a difficult prayer to truly mean, but well worth the risk!

The third way I see the term alignment is in the physical sense. I have struggled most of my life with a curvature in my spine. This curve has caused many peripheral issues alongside: pinched nerves, pressure, digestive issues, deflected pain, headaches, etc. When the spine is out of proper positioning, it can greatly effect, even paralyze the entire body. There are many natural things we can do to help align the spine: stretching, therapy, chiropractic adjustments have all been very effective for me. In proper alignment, I stand taller, thinner, stronger, and more energetic in life. The key is that a quick snap in place adjustment may help for the moment, but continual strengthening and stretching is what it takes to maintain proper alignment.

As in all three of these aspects, our spiritual alignment is critical to healthy living in our post. Are our relationships in Kingdom order, and are we honoring those whom God has placed in our lives? Is our lifestyle in line with the Kingdom of God and who we are called to be? In all the areas where we get off track and out of balance, are we allowing the Holy Spirit to come in and make the necessary adjustments to keep us standing straight and tall, stronger and with more vitality? Do we strengthen ourselves in the Word, His Presence and in discipleship, allowing God to stretch us in order to maintain proper alignment? Evaluate your spiritual "spinal condition" seeing the areas of weakness that are bringing unnecessary difficulty to other areas of your life.

Sometimes, as with the chiropractor, we need God to just snap us back into alignment. He may use trials, other people, His Word, times in His presence, and endless other tools to do so. Let us not be so quick to utilize all our efforts to blame the enemy when we are feeling uncomfortable in life. It may be that God is pressing in on us, to stretch us, shape us, strengthen us, and ultimately align us for His destined post!

Then, our job kicks in! On a daily basis, we need to maintain that aligning work. Get into the presence of God. There's nothing like the weight of His glory to press you into alignment! If you are transparently exposing yourself to His presence, the Refiner's Fire will come and re-align you to the new creation reality, the mighty soldier prepared to command your post!

Every single day, recognize the distractions in your life that come to rob you. Recognize distractions and adjust. Doors close and doors open. Adjust. Tune in to the voice of the Spirit, and adjust accordingly. Be sensitive to when you are veering off course, then adjust. Sense when your heart is not right; adjust. Know when your priorities are upside-down, and adjust.

Most of all, feel when we are straying away from His presence, adjust and come home. Keep adjusting and you'll maintain your alignment; your posture will be strengthened, you'll be standing powerful in the full armor of God, ready to command your post!

Philippians 3:12: *"Not that I have now attained [this ideal], or have already been made perfect, but I press on to lay hold of (grasp) and make my own, that for which Christ Jesus (the Messiah) has laid hold of me and made me His own."* (Amplified Version)

Our post is ours to grasp, and it comes through a series of courageous choices. To choose more rather than less. You have a choice to act, not based on your emotions, rationale, circumstances, or other's opinions but based on your destiny. Step out. Because God is calling your name, you can step off that cliff. It is a risk but you have a choice. Will you risk it all for the sake of a God-sized call?

It's time for you to ultimately actualize something within the territory that God has for your life. Functioning within these parameters, whether moral, ethical or just specific to you, brings blessings, assurance, protection, and covenant promises that come to pass with supernatural provision.

Years ago, as I went to the Word in my quiet time before Him, He led me to my own personal statement of faith. This statement has carried me through incredibly difficult seasons and has guarded and kept me in my post.

I Believe that ...
> You are all that You say You are,
>> That You will do all that You said You would do,
>> & that You reign over all!

This encapsulates my faith in a tangible manner. When emotions erupt, when circumstances bring confusion, when others disappoint, and life becomes overwhelming, I cling to this proclamation!

We are living in a day of Kingdom advancement. If we do not take up our post, we are slowing the progress and allowing the enemy to take more territory in the world. There has never been a day in history that is in such vital need of the church to arise. The time is critical ...

**Find your post, command it!**
**Your post is God-dreamed,**
**it's God-defined and it's God-disclosed just for you.**

**Find that position,**
**discover your passions**
**and align that posture**
**for you have a post to command**
**in this day of Kingdom advancement!**

## Bibliography

**The Amplified Bible**
Frances E. Siewert, ed., The Amplified Bible. Grand Rapids: Zondervan, 1965. Revised 1987.

**The Message Bible**
Eugene H. Peterson, The Message: The Bible in Contemporary Language. Colorado Springs: NavPress, 2002.

**Ten - How Would You Rate Your Life?**
Smith, Terry (2012-01-02). Ten -- How Would You Rate Your Life? (p. 47). HigherLife Development Services, Inc.. Kindle Edition.

**Hosting the Presence: Unveiling Heaven's Agenda**
Johnson, Bill (2012-05-15). Hosting the Presence: Unveiling Heaven's Agenda (p. 151). Destiny Image. Kindle Edition.

**When Heaven Invades Earth**
Johnson, Bill (2005-01-28). When Heaven Invades Earth (pp. 90-91). Destiny Image. Kindle Edition.

**Oxford Dictionary**
www.oxforddictionaries.com

**Dressed to Kill**
Renner, Rick (2012-12-18). Dressed to Kill: A Biblical Approach to Spiritual Warfare and Armor (Kindle Locations 1936-1937). Harrison House Publishers. Kindle Edition.

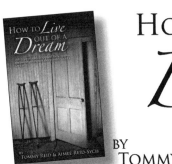

# HOW TO *Live* *D*OUT OF A *Dream*

BY
## TOMMY REID & AIMEE REID-SYCH

## ORDER FORM

Quantity: _____ books x $14.95 ea. = Subtotal:    $ _____

Shipping & Handling add 10% ($4 minimum):    $ _____

New York State sales tax (if applicable)    $ _____

Total    $ _____

**Make checks Payable to COVnet Ministries. U.S. Funds, please.**

**Shipping Address:**

Name: _____

Address: _____

City, State, Zip: _____

Mail this completed order form together with payment to:
**KAIROS Resource Center**
3210 Southwestern Blvd.
Orchard Park, NY 14127

For quantity discounts and MasterCard/VISA, or international
orders, call 1-800-52wings, or order on dreammydestiny.com or
www.kairosresourcecenter.com

## ORDER FORM

---

## Tommy Reid DVDs and Books

### DVD Order

*How To Live Out of a Dream* : Qty _____ x $15 ea. = Subtotal: $ _____

*Journal Of Life* : Qty _____ x $10 ea. = Subtotal: $ _____

### Book Order

Kingdom Now But Not Yet: Qty _____ x $10 ea. = Subtotal: $ _____

The Exploding Church: Qty _____ x $10 ea. = Subtotal: $ _____

**SPECIAL:** Save $10 by purchasing ALL FOUR Items

Both DVDs and both books: Qty _____ x $35 ea. = Subtotal: $ _____

## Aimee Reid-Sych DVDs

*Release The Sound* : Qty _____ x $15 ea. = Subtotal: $ _____

*Passion for His Presence* : Qty _____ x $15 ea. = Subtotal: $ _____

**SPECIAL:** Save $10 by purchasing both DVDs

Both DVDs Qty _____ x $20 ea. = Subtotal: $ _____

---

Shipping & Handling add 10% ($4 minimum): $ _____

New York State sales tax (if applicable) $ _____

**Total** $ _____

## Order today through:

### KAIROS Resource Center

www.kairosresourcecenter.com

3210 Southwestern Blvd., Orchard Park, NY 14127

**Make checks payable to COVnet Ministries. (U.S. Funds, please)**

### Shipping Address:

Name: _____

Address: _____

City, State, Zip: _____

Mail this completed order form, together with payment, to:

### KAIROS Resource Center

3210 Southwestern Blvd., Orchard Park, NY 14127

### How to Live out of a Dream

This is an amazing docu-drama of the events in the life of a great dreamer. In these fast-moving forty minutes, you will see the healing of a boy crippled by polio. This boy learned to dream as he heard the voice of Jesus speak to him. and then took the hand of the One who would lead him through his life. See his mother as teaching him to dream, and the unbelievable story of ten-year-old Paul Crouch encouraging Tommy that he can do anything if he will just believe. Come take a journey with a dreamer as he teaches you to dream.

### DVD - $15

### Journal of Life

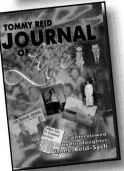

Tommy Reid is interviewed by his daughter Aimee, and shares with her the story of his fifty-plus years of ministry. You will see his early ministry in the Philippines, as the young 26-year-old Tommy becomes pastor of the great Bethel Temple in Manila. See 31-year-old Tommy, work with Dr. Cho spending their first year ministering together in what will later grow to become the largest church in the world. Revisit, with sight and sound, the tent meetings of the 1950's, the amazing miracles of healing around the world, the great Charismatic renewal, and the Jesus movement in Buffalo during the 1960's.

### DVD - $10

### Kingdom Now, But not yet

This is classic Tommy Reid as he shares the Biblical concept of bringing the wonder of the reign of Christ to the world in every day life. *Kingdom Now, But not yet* has inspired great ministries in many nations to change their world. If you want to be a world changer, *Kingdom Now, But not yet* is a must for you.

### Book - $10

### The Exploding Church

*The Exploding Church* is the amazing story of a  church that grew from 120 attendees to over 800 in a single week. This was a runaway best seller in its day, making Tommy Reid one of the best known speakers in the world in the 1960's and 1970's. Hundreds of churches across the world were inspired by this story as it became a church growth classic in the 1970's.

### Book - $10

## *Release the Sound*

Imagine with us waves of sound arising from the hearts of the people of God. This sound is a Heavenly anthem, the sound of the Kingdom! In natural sound, two frequencies traveling toward each other from opposite directions will produce an amplitude twice their size when they meet. When our worship joins Heaven's song, the two become a single, pure, supernatural anthem with twice the amplitude, twice the reach! Our worship, joined with the worship of Heaven releases a sound over our cities, our nation, our world. We invite you to journey with us to Release the Sound of the Kingdom and become a partner with God as His Kingdom revolution takes place!

**CD $15**

## *Passion for His Presence*

True worship strives to live at a level of perfect intimacy with the Lord of All - it is all that we are openly communicating with the Spirit of God! It is for worship that we were created. Once true worship begins to unfold in our lives, we develop a passion for God that burns in our heart of hearts! He so deeply desires to have an amazing and intimate relationship with you; true worship leads you into this intimacy. It opens the doors to heaven, to eternity. All that you long for in eternity can be born in your life today through worship.

**CD $15**